CONTENTS

INTRODUCTION

Spring is a time of new life and new energy on the Eckert family farms. During the cold midwestern winters, as the orchards rest in dormancy and our gardens are but mere plots of land waiting to be tended, we long for the spring harvest. As the days begin to lengthen and the temperatures climb, we start our tasks of carefully pruning, plowing, and planting on the farm and in our home gardens. These duties may seem mundane to some, but for us, they signify the hope of the bounty of the seasons ahead.

As the spring harvest finally draws near, we enthusiastically begin to prepare for recipes—new and old—featuring the season's freshest ingredients, including asparagus, strawberries, spring onions, garlic, and a plethora of herbs. As always, our goal is to highlight the naturally delicious flavors of fresh, seasonal ingredients. We do this daily, in our homes for our families and in our cooking classroom, by preparing a variety of sweet and savory preparations using the long-awaited spring bounty.

Through *The Eckert Family Spring Cookbook*, we share our passion for growing and preparing the fresh flavors of spring. Similar to our Summer and Fall cookbooks, the Spring cookbook includes traditional recipes from our German ancestors as well as more modern recipes developed and tested in our cooking classroom.

The Eckert family has been growing fruit since 1837. Generations of Eckert children grew up eager to help on the farm and in Grandma's garden. They anxiously awaited the peach and apple bloom as the perfect time to play in the orchard. Springtime also meant family days of toiling in the fields and making sweet jam in the kitchen. These traditions continue within the Eckert family and on its farms and home gardens, which grow a diversity of fruits and vegetables.

The Eckert family delights in using fresh, seasonally and locally grown foods for its recipes, and each year, spring marks the first harvest of homegrown goodness.

APPETIZERS & DRINKS

— From Our Family Album —

After selling fruit out of the back of a horse-drawn wagon for ten years, Alvin Eckert made a leap into more permanent retail in the mid-1920s. He rented a stone storefront on the corner of Mascoutah Avenue and Greenmount Road to sell his fresh produce.

Roasted Asparagus with Prosciutto Ham

2½ lb. medium asparagus spears, trimmed

2 Tbs. olive oil

½ tsp. salt

¼ tsp. ground black pepper

3 oz. prosciutto ham, cut in half lengthwise

Preheat oven to 500°F. Toss asparagus with oil, salt and pepper in a shallow oven-proof baking pan. Wrap a piece of ham around two spears of uncooked asparagus. Arrange wrapped asparagus in a single layer and place pan in oven. Bake 10 to 14 minutes or until lightly brown and fork-tender, turning asparagus about half way through roasting. Makes 5 to 6 servings.

—— From Our Family Album ——

In the early 1900s, Grandpa Alvin Eckert grew white asparagus in the garden area next to the "house on the hill" that still stands on our Belleville Farm. Alvin covered the white asparagus crowns with mounds of soil before the the tips emerged from the ground.

Grilled Italian Cheese

8 oz. cream cheese
¼ cup basil pesto (recipe on p. 26)
1 unpeeled plum tomato, chopped
¼ cup shredded mozzarella
Crackers or Eckert's bakery bread slices for serving

Heat grill to medium heat. Unwrap cream cheese and place on 8-inch square sheet of heavy-duty foil; top with pesto, chopped plum tomato and mozzarella cheese. Leave foil open and place foil on grill; close grill lid. Grill 8 to 10 minutes or until shredded cheese is melted and cream cheese is softened, but still holding shape. Transfer foil to platter. Serve spread with crackers or bread. Makes 10 to 12 servings.

NOTE: Prepare this recipe year-round by baking in a preheated 375°F oven for 12 to 14 minutes.

Strawberry Flatbread

4 to 5 cups fresh strawberries, hulled and sliced

1 Tbs. aged balsamic vinegar

½ tsp. fresh ground black pepper

1 to 2 tsp. granulated sugar, optional

5 to 6 pieces flat bread

2 large balls fresh mozzarella cheese, sliced thin

2 to 3 Tbs. fresh basil ribbons

Gently combine balsamic vinegar, black pepper, and strawberries. Cover and marinate for at least 30 minutes at room temperature. Preheat broiler to 400°F. When ready to serve, taste strawberry mixture and adjust seasonings with granulated sugar, if necessary. Cover each piece of flatbread with slices of mozzarella cheese. Broil until cheese melts, about 1 to 2 minutes. Cut into wedges. Top with strawberry mixture. Garnish with fresh basil. Makes 5 to 6 servings.

Chicken, Spinach and Artichoke Melts

4 Tbs. butter

1 garlic clove, minced

1 Tbs. all-purpose flour

½ cup milk (skim, 2% or whole)

1 oz. cream cheese

½ cup shredded mozzarella cheese

½ cup grated Parmesan cheese

½ cup plain Greek yogurt

½ tsp. black pepper

½ cup (about 5 oz.) frozen, chopped, spinach, thawed

1 jar (about 7 oz.) marinated artichoke hearts

1 chicken breast, grilled and sliced thin or 8 oz. sliced deli meat

8 slices of Eckert's Farm Bread or Eckert's Sourdough Bread

Melt 1 tablespoon of butter in a skillet over medium heat. Add garlic and cook for 2 minutes. Whisk in flour until it makes a paste. Reduce heat to medium-low and cook for 1 to 2 more minutes, then add milk. Stir and cook 2 more minutes. (If paste is too thick to stir, add a few more drops of milk.) Stir in three cheeses and black pepper. Add Greek yogurt and stir until smooth. Add artichokes and spinach and stir to combine, remove from heat. (Mixture will be thick.) Butter one side of each bread slice. On unbuttered sides, spread 2 tablespoons of artichoke/spinach mixture and top with chicken. Place remaining bread slices on chicken, buttered side up. Heat a skillet or griddle over medium heat. Place four sandwiches in skillet and cook until each side is golden and cheese is melted. Makes 4 "melts" with extra spread.

NOTE: Remaining spinach artichoke spread makes an excellent sauce for pasta or a hot dip for chips or bread.

Antipasti Bites

24 thin slices of hard or Genoa salami (about 4 inches in diameter)

1 cup marinated artichoke hearts, chopped fine

½ cup roasted red peppers, chopped fine

4 oz. fresh mozzarella, cut into small cubes

½ cup fresh basil, chopped

Press one salami slice down into a regular sized muffin cup in a muffin tin. Bake at 400°F for approximately 10 minutes or until salami is crisp. Transfer salami to a plate to cool. Combine remaining ingredients and spoon into salami cups to serve. Makes 24 pieces.

Cheesy Herb Bread

1 unsliced round loaf of Eckert's sourdough or Eckert's White Mountain Bread

16 oz. mozzarella cheese slices

4 Tbs. fresh herbs or 1½ tsp. dried herbs

2 large peaches, peeled and sliced

Cut the top of bread in a grid-like pattern, making cuts every 2 inches without cutting through the bottom crust. Insert cheese between cuts. Combine butter and herbs. Drizzle over the bread. Wrap in foil; place on a baking sheet. Bake at 350°F for 15 minutes. Unwrap; bake 10 minutes longer or until the cheese is melted. Makes 8 servings.

Sweet Strawberry Bruschetta

4 slices French bread, cut into ½ to ¾ inch thickness

6 Tbs. light brown sugar

1 tsp. grated lemon zest

2 tsp. fresh-squeezed lemon juice

3 cups strawberries, hulled and diced

4 Tbs. goat cheese, at room temperature

4 Tbs. of Eckert's Pure Honey

Toast bread. Heat medium skillet over high heat. Add brown sugar, lemon zest, and juice; cook, stirring constantly until sugar melts and mixture begins to bubble, about 1 to 2 minutes. Add strawberries and stir until juices begin to release and berries are just starting to heat, about 30 seconds. Remove immediately from heat. Spread 1 tablespoon goat cheese on each piece of toast. Top with warm berries. Drizzle with honey. Makes 4 servings.

Champagne Strawberry Soup

2 cups strawberries, sliced

1 cup orange juice

16 oz. strawberry yogurt

1 Tbs. granulated sugar

½ tsp. vanilla extract

¾ cup champagne or dry white wine, chilled (white grape juice may be substituted)

8 whole strawberries for garnish

Place all ingredients except champagne and whole strawberries in blender container; blend until smooth. Chill. Just before serving, stir in champagne. Garnish with additional strawberries, if desired. Makes 8 servings (about ½ cup each).

Five Herb Cheese Spread

1 peeled clove garlic

2 (8 oz.) packages cream cheese, softened

1 cup butter, softened

¼ tsp. dried or ¾ tsp. fresh basil

¼ tsp. dried or ¾ tsp. fresh marjoram

¼ tsp. ground black pepper

1 tsp. dried or 1 Tbs. fresh oregano

¼ tsp. dried or ¾ tsp. fresh dill weed

¼ tsp. dried or ¾ tsp. fresh thyme

In a food processor, chop garlic finely. Add cream cheese and remaining ingredients, process until smooth, stopping to scrape down sides. Shape into balls ¾ inches in diameter. Cover and store in refrigerator until ready to use. Spread on crackers or baguette bread or melt on steaks or vegetables. Makes 3 cups.

Moscato Strawberry Slushes

1 750-ml bottle sweet, uncarbonated Moscato wine, divided

2 cups strawberries, hulled

1 Tbs. fresh lemon juice

1 Tbs. sugar

Measure out 1 cup of wine into a container and refrigerate. Puree the remaining wine with all remaining ingredients in a food processor. Pour the mixture into ice cube trays and freeze until solid. When ready to serve, puree ice cubes with chilled wine in a blender. Makes 6 servings.

Strawberry Refresher

2 cups orange juice (freshly squeezed preferred), chilled

2 cups strawberries, hulled and mashed

1 Tbs. super fine sugar

1½ cups ginger ale, chilled

1 tsp. finely grated fresh ginger root

Whole strawberries for garnish

Sliced oranges, cut in half for garnish

Combine juice, strawberries, and granulated sugar in blender container, blend until berries are pureed. Place berry puree in pitcher. Add ginger ale and ginger; stir for 1 to 2 seconds to combine. Garnish with sliced oranges. Refrigerate until serving. Makes 4 servings.

--- *From Our Kitchen* ---

To make super fine sugar, place 1 cup granulated sugar into a blender. Blend until sugar is fine, about 1 minute. Store in air tight container.

Old-Fashion Pink Lemonade

2 large lemons at room temperature

1½ cups water

⅓ cup granulated sugar

1 cup strawberries, hulled and sliced

2 large whole strawberries for garnish

Ice cubes as needed (optional)

Cut lemons in half across the middle. Using a citrus juicer, squeeze the juice from each half. You should have about ½ cup juice. Pour the lemon juice into a pitcher. Add water and granulated sugar. Stir until the granulated sugar is dissolved. Set a fine-mesh sieve over a small bowl. Put the strawberry slices in the sieve and mash with the back of a small spoon, pushing the berries through the sieve. Discard seeds. Pour the strained strawberries into the lemonade. Stir the lemonade until well blended and pink. Cover and refrigerate until well chilled. To serve, fill glasses with ice cubes and then pour in the lemonade. Garnish with whole strawberries. Makes 2 servings.

Strawberry-Basil Lemonade

2 cups strawberries, hulled and diced, plus extra for garnish

3 cups water, divided

1 cup plus 2 Tbs. granulated sugar

Zest of one lemon

½ cup fresh tightly packed basil leaves, plus extra for garnish (garnish optional)

1½ cups fresh lemon juice (from about 6 lemons)

Ice cubes

1 cup vodka (optional)

Combine strawberries and 2 tablespoons of the sugar. Set aside. In a small pot with a lid, combine 1 cup water, remaining 1 cup sugar, the lemon zest and basil over medium-high heat. Stir until sugar is dissolved, about 5 to 6 minutes to create a syrup. Cover, remove from heat and steep 10 minutes. Strain syrup. Discard zest and basil and allow remaining syrup to cool. In a pitcher, stir together strawberries, lemon juice, syrup, 2 cups ice and 2 cups cold water. (For an adult beverage, replace 1 cup of the water with 1 cup vodka.) Fill 8 glasses with ice and lemonade. Garnish with extra strawberries and basil, if desired. Makes 8 servings.

Honey Mint Iced Tea

4 cups boiling water
½ cup fresh mint leaves, washed
2 green or black tea bags
¼ cup Eckert's Pure Honey

In a large heat-proof pitcher, pour boiling water over mint and tea bags. Whisk in honey. Let steep 5 minutes. Remove tea bags; cool. Refrigerate until ready to serve. When ready to serve, pour over ice. Makes 4 servings.

—— *From Our Family Album* ——

Grandma Eckert hated snakes! She once killed a garden snake with a hoe and stretched it out on a picnic table to show off her handy work.

SALADS

—— *From Our Family Album* ——

Upon the completion of a road that is now called Route 15, Alvin built a new retail facility and moved his operations to his home farm. This began a 90-year tradition of retail operations on this once humble, rural corner.

Strawberry Salad
with Creamy Poppy Seed Dressing

1 head romaine or red tipped
lettuce

1 pint (2 cups) strawberries, hulled
and sliced

1 small red onion, thinly sliced

1 garlic scape, pod and tip removed,
diced (optional)

½ cup mayonnaise

2 Tbs. strawberry vinegar (see next
recipe), or a light wine vinegar

⅓ cup granulated sugar

¼ cup whole milk

2 Tbs. poppy seeds

Wash lettuce and spin or pat dry. Refrigerate until
serving. Place greens in large salad bowl. Arrange
berries, onion and diced scape sliced on top
of greens. Place remaining ingredients in a jar.
Cover and shake until blended. Drizzle dressing
over top and toss gently. Makes 6 servings.

Strawberry Vinegar for Salad Dressings

2 cups fresh strawberries, sliced
1 quart canning jar, lid and ring
2 cups white wine vinegar
¼ cup granulated sugar
2 (8 oz.) canning jars
2 lids and rings

Place strawberries in a clean 1-quart jar. Press strawberries inside jar with a wooden spoon to release juices. Set aside. Combine vinegar and granulated sugar in a 2-quart stainless steel saucepan. Bring to a boil; reduce heat, and simmer until sugar dissolves, about 1 to 2 minutes. Pour vinegar mixture over strawberries in quart jar. Allow to cool about 30 minutes. Cover with flat lid and ring. Let stand at room temperature for 48 hours. Wash remaining 8-ounce canning jars in hot soapy water. Rinse well. Place jars in a pan of boiling water, enough to cover jar. Reduce heat to simmer. Leave jars in water until ready to use. Strain vinegar mixture through a cheesecloth or paper towel-lined sieve; discard strawberry pulp. Place vinegar mixture in a medium stainless steel saucepan. Bring to a boil; boil 2 minutes. Cool; pour into 8-ounce jars. Store in refrigerator 5 to 6 months.
Makes about 2 cups.

Berry Green Salad
with Vinaigrette Poppy Seed Dressing

DRESSING
½ cup granulated sugar
¾ tsp. dry mustard
¾ tsp. salt
¼ cup white wine vinegar
⅔ cup vegetable oil
1 Tbs. poppy seeds

SALAD
¼ cup pecan halves
4 tsp. granulated sugar
6 cups mixed greens, washed and dried
2 ribs celery, chopped
2 green onions, sliced thin
1 cup strawberries, sliced
1 cup blueberries

TO PREPARE DRESSING: Mix together granulated sugar, dry mustard, salt and vinegar. Whisk in oil and poppy seeds; blend well.

TO PREPARE SALAD: Toast the pecans in a frying pan over medium heat, about 2 to 3 minutes. Add the granulated sugar and heat until pecans are coated, about 2 minutes. Let cool and break apart. Place greens in a large salad bowl. Top with pecans, celery, onion and fruit. Drizzle with dressing. Makes 4 to 6 servings.

Eckert's Pick Your Own Salad

DRESSING
2 large eggs beaten
½ cup apple cider vinegar
1 cup granulated sugar
1 tsp. salt
1 tsp. dry mustard

SALAD
8 cups red or green leaf lettuce, washed, dried and torn into bite-size pieces
2 Eckert's spring onions, thinly sliced
2 cups sliced strawberries, blueberries and blackberries
½ cup sliced almonds, chopped pecans, or chopped walnuts

TO PREPARE DRESSING: Combine ingredients in a heavy saucepan over medium heat. Stir constantly with whisk until dressing comes to a boil, about 3 to 4 minutes. Allow dressing to cool. Cover and refrigerate until serving.

TO PREPARE SALAD: Combine all ingredients on a large platter or in a large salad bowl. Drizzle cold dressing on top. Toss gently. Makes 6 servings.

From Our Kitchen

Eckert's Pick Your Own Salad is a family favorite especially for Easter gatherings. We make many variations of this recipe throughout the year using seasonal fruits and nuts.

SALADS

Chicken Salad with Pesto Vinaigrette

PESTO VINAIGRETTE
¼ cup white wine vinegar
¼ cup extra-virgin olive oil
1 Tbs. pesto (see recipe on p. 26)
2 tsp. fresh lemon juice
1 tsp. whole-grain Dijon mustard
½ tsp. salt
¼ tsp. ground black pepper

CHICKEN SALAD
3 cups chopped cooked chicken
1 cup cored and chopped tomato
½ cup chopped black olives
½ cup chopped artichoke hearts
¼ cup toasted walnuts
4 slices Eckert's Hummingbird
bread or 4 lettuce leaves

TO PREPARE PESTO VINAIGRETTE: In a small bowl, whisk together vinegar, oil, pesto, lemon juice, mustard, salt, and pepper. Cover and chill.

TO PREPARE SALAD: In a medium bowl, combine chicken, tomato, olives, artichokes and walnuts. Add the Pesto Vinaigrette, tossing gently to coat. Serve immediately open face on bread or on top of a lettuce leaf. Makes 4 servings.

Pasta, Tuna, and Roasted Pepper Salad

6 oz. uncooked pasta

5 oz. can solid white tuna in water, drained

8 oz. jar roasted red bell peppers, rinsed and sliced (¾ cup), divided

½ cup finely chopped red onion

2 Tbs. nonpareil capers, rinsed

2 Tbs. nonfat plain yogurt

2 Tbs. chopped fresh basil

1 Tbs. extra-virgin olive oil

1½ tsp. lemon juice

1 small garlic clove, crushed and peeled

⅛ tsp. salt, or to taste

Freshly ground pepper to taste

Cook pasta according to package directions, drain and set aside to cool. Combine tuna, ⅓ cup red peppers, onion, and capers in a large bowl. Set aside. Combine yogurt, basil, oil, lemon juice, garlic, salt, pepper and remaining ⅓ cup red peppers in a blender or food processor. Puree until smooth. Add pasta to the tuna mixture along with the red pepper sauce; toss to coat. Serve immediately or refrigerate.

Makes 4 servings.

Arugula Salad with Almonds & Prosciutto

⅓ cup toasted almonds

3 Tbs. olive oil

2 tsp. fresh lemon juice

2 tsp. balsamic vinegar

Coarse kosher salt and ground pepper

5 to 6 cups arugula

⅓ cup shaved Parmesan cheese, plus more for serving

4 thin slices prosciutto ham, julienned

In a large salad bowl, whisk almonds, oil, lemon juice, and vinegar; season with salt and pepper. Add arugula and Parmesan and toss to coat. Top with prosciutto and more Parmesan just before serving. Makes 4 servings.

BLT and Poached Egg Salad

VINAIGRETTE
1 tsp. Dijon mustard
1 tsp. minced shallot
¼ tsp. granulated sugar
2½ tsp. salt, divided
4 Tbs. white wine vinegar, divided
3 Tbs. extra virgin olive oil

SALAD
6 slices thick-cut uncooked bacon, coarsely chopped
3 large peeled or unpeeled tomatoes, chopped
3 Tbs. fresh basil leaves, torn
4 cups butter leaf lettuce leaves, torn
2 tsp. salt
4 large uncooked eggs

TO PREPARE VINAIGRETTE: Whisk mustard, shallot, sugar, ½ teaspoon salt, and 2 tablespoons of vinegar in a small bowl. Let the mixture sit 10 minutes, then whisk in the oil.

TO PREPARE SALAD: Heat a skillet over medium heat. Add the chopped bacon and sauté until most of the fat is rendered and the bacon is crisp on the edges but still chewy at the center, about 5 minutes. Transfer bacon to a paper towel-lined plate to drain. Discard drippings. In a large bowl, combine the tomatoes, basil, lettuce and bacon. Drizzle on 2 tablespoons of the vinaigrette to taste. Divide the salad among 4 individual plates.

Fill a saucepan pan with 1½ inches water and bring to a boil. Reduce the heat to a gentle simmer, and stir in the remaining 2 tablespoons of vinegar and 2 teaspoons of salt. Working quickly, one at a time, crack the eggs into a small bowl and slide them into the simmering water. Use a spoon to direct the egg white closer to the yolk. Raise the heat briefly to return the water to a simmer but do not allow it to boil. Poach until the whites are set and the yolks are still soft, 3 to 4 minutes. One at a time, lift the eggs from the water with a slotted spoon, blot gently with a paper towel and then carefully place on the salads. Season the eggs with salt and pepper and serve immediately. Makes 4 servings.

Tiny Pasta with Zucchini and Peppers

Kosher salt

1¼ cup small uncooked pasta, such as farfalline or orzo

3 Tbs. olive oil, divided

1 medium carrot, diced

1 small onion, diced

2 cloves garlic, minced

¾ cup diced red or yellow bell peppers

1 medium unpeeled zucchini, diced

¼ cup dry white wine or chicken broth

3 Tbs. chopped fresh flat-leaf parsley (or 3 tsp. dried)

1 Tbs. chopped fresh oregano leaves (or 1 tsp. dried), optional

¼ cup grated Romano cheese

Freshly ground pepper

Bring a large pot of salted water to a boil and add the pasta. Cook until al dente; drain and rinse briefly under cool water. Return cooked pasta to the pot, toss with 1 tablespoon olive oil. Heat the remaining oil in a large frying pan over medium-high heat. Add the carrot and onion and cook, stirring until the onion is translucent, about 8 minutes. Turn the heat to high. Add garlic, peppers, and zucchini and sauté for another 3 to 4 minutes, watching carefully to not burn the garlic. Add wine or broth and cook over medium heat, scraping up any browned bits stuck to the bottom of the pan. Pour vegetable mixture over cooked pasta. Gently mix and season with salt and pepper to taste. Top with chopped herbs and cheese and serve. Makes 4 servings.

Spring Garden Salad with Blue Cheese

½ cup vegetable oil
¼ cup rice vinegar
1 Tbs. balsamic vinegar
2 Tbs. granulated sugar
2 tsp. butter
¾ cup walnuts, coarsely chopped
2 heads romaine lettuce washed, dried and torn
2 cups strawberries, sliced
1 cup asparagus tips, lightly blanched
½ cup crumbled blue cheese
½ cup dried cranberries

Whisk together first 4 ingredients. Set aside. Melt butter in a skillet over medium heat; add walnuts, and sauté 5 minutes or until lightly browned. Remove walnuts with a slotted spoon. Toss together lettuce, strawberries, asparagus and toasted walnuts. Sprinkle with cheese and cranberries; drizzle with dressing.
Makes 4 to 6 servings.

Grilled Spring Onion Salad

3 Tbs. olive oil, divided
8 small spring onion bulbs
½ tsp. kosher salt, divided
½ tsp. freshly ground black pepper, divided
1 Tbs. whole grain Dijon mustard
1 Tbs. red wine vinegar
2 tsp. chopped flat-leaf parsley
2 tsp. chopped fresh tarragon
4 cups mixed salad greens
12 cherry tomatoes, halved
2 hard-cooked eggs, sliced, garnish (see p. 48 for perfect hard-cooked eggs)
2 Tbs. minced fresh chives, garnish

Preheat charcoal or gas grill to medium heat. Leaving greens attached, cut onion in half, lengthwise through the bulb. Rub 1 tablespoon olive oil evenly over onions. Sprinkle evenly with ¼ teaspoon salt and ¼ teaspoon pepper. Grill onions 6 minutes or until well marked and greens are tender, turning occasionally. Cool completely. Whisk together mustard and vinegar in a small bowl. Gradually whisk in remaining 2 tablespoons oil followed by parsley, tarragon, remaining ¼ teaspoon salt, and remaining ¼ teaspoon pepper. Divide salad greens among 4 plates, top with onions and with tomatoes. Drizzle 1 tablespoon vinaigrette over each salad; garnish with sliced eggs and minced chives.
Makes 4 servings.

Honey Orange Fruit Salad Dressing

½ cup plain yogurt
¼ cup Eckert's Pure Honey
¼ cup mayonnaise
¾ tsp. grated orange peel
¼ tsp. dry mustard
3 Tbs. orange juice
1½ tsp. vinegar

Whisk together yogurt, honey, mayonnaise, orange peel, and mustard in a small bowl until blended. Gradually mix in orange juice and vinegar. Cover and refrigerate until ready to serve. Makes about 1 cup.

Serve with mixed fresh or frozen fruit salads.

Herbed Garden Salad with Goat Cheese

6 cups (6 oz.) hydroponic lettuce or salad greens
1 cup (1 oz.) mixed fresh herb leaves such as tarragon, flat-leaf parsley, dill, chervil and chives in any combination
Approximately ⅛ cup extra-virgin olive oil
Kosher salt and freshly ground pepper
¼ tsp. sugar
1 to 2 tsp. white wine vinegar
½ lb. fresh goat cheese, crumbled

In a large bowl, combine the lettuce and herbs. Drizzle with just enough oil to coat lightly and then toss. Season with salt and pepper and the sugar, and then toss the greens again. Drizzle with 1 to 2 teaspoons vinegar and toss. Taste for tanginess and adjust seasonings with salt, pepper and vinegar as needed. Sprinkle the goat cheese over the top and serve immediately. Makes 6 servings.

SAUCES, PRESERVES, & TOPPINGS

Alvin's three sons were innovative and determined to expand the Eckert business. They chose to join forces with IGA (Independent Grocers Alliance) to become a full-line grocer. One of their innovative strategies was to open for business on Sundays, long before retailers were keeping such hours.

Basic Basil Pesto

Kosher salt and ground black pepper
1 peeled clove garlic
¼ cup toasted pine nuts or walnuts
3 cups packed, fresh basil leaves
⅔ cup extra virgin olive oil, divided
½ cup freshly grated Parmesan cheese

On a cutting board, sprinkle ¼ teaspoon salt over garlic and roughly chop. Using the flat side of a knife, crush garlic mixture into a thick paste. Add paste to a food processor with nuts, basil and 1 tablespoon olive oil. Pulse until ingredients are finely chopped. With machine running, add remaining olive oil in a slow steady stream. Add Parmesan and pulse to combine. Season with salt and pepper. Makes about 1 cup.

From Our Kitchen

To store pesto, place in an airtight container with plastic wrap pressed against the surface so it doesn't oxidize and turn brown. Refrigerate up to 2 days or freeze up to 3 months.
Thaw before using.

Basil Garlic Butter

1 cup butter, softened
2 peeled garlic cloves
½ cup basil leaves, firmly packed

Process butter and garlic cloves in a food processor until smooth. Add basil leaves and pulse 3 to 4 times or until basil is finely chopped. Store in refrigerator up to 1 week or freeze. Makes about 1¼ cups.

NOTE: If desired, shape butter into log, wrap in wax paper, and chill. When firm, slice into small rounds.

From Our Kitchen

To toast nuts arrange them in one layer on a rimmed baking sheet. Toast the nuts for about 6 to 8 minutes at 350°F or until fragrant and slightly browned. Let cool, then coarsely chop.

Basil Rouille Bruschetta

1 cup snipped (fresh) basil

1 tomato, seeded and chopped, peeled (optional)

⅓ cup fine dry bread crumbs

4 large peeled garlic cloves, minced

1 tsp. kosher salt

½ cup olive oil

10 to 12 baguette slices

½ to ¾ cup shredded mozzarella cheese

In bowl, stir together basil, tomato, crumbs, garlic, and salt. Gradually add oil and mix well. Slice baguette, brush both sides with olive oil and place under broiler to toast, a few minutes per side. Spoon about 1 teaspoon of basil mixture onto each piece of bread, sprinkle with cheese, and broil just until cheese begins to melt, about 2 minutes. Makes 10 to 12 pieces.

NOTE: Rouille may be made ahead and stored in the refrigerator. Bring to room temperature before spreading on toasted bread.

Cilantro Pesto

½ cup loosely packed, fresh cilantro leaves

½ cup loosely packed, fresh flat-leaf parsley leaves

2 peeled garlic cloves

¼ cup freshly grated Parmesan cheese

2 Tbs. walnuts or pumpkin seeds, toasted

¼ tsp. salt

¼ cup olive oil

Pulse the first 6 ingredients in a food processor until just chopped, about 10 times. Drizzle olive oil over mixture and pulse 6 more times or until a coarse mixture forms. Cover and chill up to 24 hours. Serve on steaks or potatoes or spread on Eckert's fresh bakery bread. Makes about ¾ cup.

—— From Our Family Album ——

Uncle Cornell lived east of Freeburg, Illinois, in Fayetteville. He and Harry Mae hosted Easter in the 1970s for the Eckert family. Eckert children especially loved playing with their miniature, cast iron stove.

Quick Herb Spread

1 cup packed, fresh basil leaves, chopped fine

1 cup mayonnaise

¼ cup packed, fresh flat-leaf parsley leaves, chopped fine

2 scallions (white and light green parts), coarsely chopped

1 large peeled garlic clove, minced (about 1½ tsp.)

1 tsp. grated lemon zest

Kosher salt and freshly ground black pepper

Combine basil, mayonnaise, parsley, scallions, garlic, and lemon zest in a blender and puree until very smooth. Add salt and pepper to taste. Cover and refrigerate until ready to serve with sandwiches, tuna fish, or on fresh steamed vegetables. Makes 1½ cups.

Balsamic Strawberries

¼ cup granulated sugar, to taste

¼ cup aged balsamic vinegar

2 tsp. freshly grated orange zest

1 tsp. orange flavored liqueur (optional)

5 cups strawberries, sliced

Mix together first 3 ingredients and liqueur if using. Pour over strawberries. Allow to strawberries to stand 10 minutes at room temperature. Serve over Eckert's Frozen Custard, cheesecake, or angel food cake. Makes about 5 cups.

Eckert's Strawberry Rhubarb Sauce

2½ cups rhubarb, trimmed and cut into ¼ inch pieces

¾ cup granulated sugar plus 1 to 2 Tbs. if needed

½ cup water

3 to 4 cups strawberries, sliced

Fresh mint leaves for garnish, optional

Whole strawberries for garnish

In a medium saucepan, combine rhubarb, granulated sugar and water. Bring to a simmer over medium-low heat and cook 8 to 10 minutes. Add sliced strawberries and cook until the rhubarb is tender and translucent, about 5 to 6 more minutes. Remove from heat and cool slightly. Using an immersion blender or food processor, puree mixture. Taste and adjust sugar. Serve warm over Eckert's Pound Cake, Eckert's Frozen Custard, pancakes, or waffles. Garnish with fresh mint leaves and a large whole strawberry, cut in half. Makes about 3 cups.

Fresh Strawberry Jam

4 (8 oz.) canning jars
4 canning lids and rings
1½ quarts fresh strawberries, hulled
6 cups granulated sugar
1 small chilled saucer

Wash jars in hot, soapy water. Rinse well. Place jars in a pan of hot boiling water. Reduce heat to simmer. Leave jars in hot water while preparing jam. Wash, drain, and hull strawberries, crush in a kettle. Stir in granulated sugar. Cook slowly stirring constantly until granulated sugar dissolves. Bring to a boil and cook rapidly until mixture thickens, stirring frequently (about 35 minutes). Do not overcook; jam thickens as it cools. Check for thickness by spooning 1 or 2 tablespoons cooked jam onto a cold saucer. Cook only until jam will round up and get slightly thick. Drain hot canning jars. Ladle immediately into hot canning jars; fill to ⅛ inch of top. With damp paper towel, wipe off rims. Screw on lids evenly and tightly, invert for a few seconds, and then stand up right to cool. Store in refrigerator and use within 4 weeks. Makes about 4 (8 oz.) jars.

—— *From Our Kitchen* ——

Jam contains crushed fruit. Preserves contain whole fruit or chunks of fruit.

Eckert's

Always in Season™

Strawberries

Strawberry season is short and sweet. The first berries typically ripen in May and the season continues into June, normally lasting about 3 weeks. The crop is planted in the fall, using transplants grown from strawberry shoots planted in nursery trays off-site. We sow the transplants into the ground in early September and allow them to grow with no protection until the first frost. After that, we cover the crop with lightweight fabric blankets to prevent them from being injured by severe cold temperatures during the winter. In the spring, once the temperatures are consistently warm enough, we remove the covers and let the plants bloom. The plants produce their first strawberries about 30 days after bloom.

STRAWBERRY EQUIVALENTS

1 qt. = 1¼ to 1½ lbs. = 2 pt.

1 qt. = approximately 48 medium strawberries

1 qt. = 4 cups whole berries, 3½ cups sliced berries, or 2½ cups pureed berries

SELECTING—Strawberries should be completely red with a bright green cap. Avoid picking strawberries with white tips or green areas; leave these for picking a day or two later.

STORING—Strawberries should be stored in shallow containers in refrigeration for no longer than 1 week. Cover loosely to help preserve humidity. Do not wash berries until you are ready to use them.

FREEZING—Wash, stem, and drain fresh strawberries. Slice into a bowl and add sugar (to 1 quart berries and add ¾ cup sugar). Immediately spoon strawberries into freezer containers, leaving headspace, then seal and freeze.

Rhubarb

Rhubarb is really a vegetable, but it is treated more like a fruit and used mainly for desserts, pies, or preserves. The stalk is the only edible part of rhubarb. The leaves are poisonous and should not be eaten.

RHUBARB EQUIVALENTS

1 lb. of raw rhubarb should yield approximately 3 cups chopped or 2 cups cooked

SELECTING—Stalks should be firm and crisp. Color is not always an indicator of ripeness because rhubarb can vary from mostly red to mostly green.

STORING—Fresh rhubarb may be stored in the refrigerator for up to 2 weeks if wrapped tightly in plastic wrap.

RHUBARB-STRAWBERRY JAM

1 cup cooked red-stalked rhubarb (about 1 lb. rhubarb and ¼ cup water)

2½ cups crushed strawberries

6½ cups sugar

1 pouch liquid pectin

To prepare fruit: Wash and chop rhubarb stalks into ¼-inch pieces. Add water, cover, and simmer about 1 to 2 minutes. Wash strawberries, remove stems and caps. Crush berries.

Place prepared rhubarb and strawberries into a heavy sauce pan. Add sugar and stir until sugar is dissolved. Place on high heat and stir constantly, bringing mixture quickly to a full boil with bubbles over the entire surface. Boil hard for 1 minute, stirring constantly. Remove from heat and stir in pectin. Fill jelly jars, leaving ¼-inch headspace. Process in a hot water canner.

Asparagus

Asparagus is an early spring crop that gets our homegrown season started. This versatile vegetable can be used in countless recipes. White asparagus is popular in Germany, and being proud of our German heritage, we feature home-grown white asparagus, as well as green asparagus. Every season, we debate which is best—white or green asparagus—with blind tastings and recipe challenges, but we will let you decide for yourself which one you prefer.

SELECTING—Select asparagus spears that are firm to the touch. The stalks should not be limp or dry on the fresh-cut end. The tips should be closed tightly and not yellowish or dried out. The diameter is not an indicator of taste, but rather a personal preference. It is more important to choose stalks of uniform thickness for control in the cooking process.

STORING—Asparagus should be stored upright in a refrigerator, with the stalks in water and the tips covered with a plastic bag.

WHITE ASPARAGUS—Growing white asparagus requires preventing the spear from being exposed to sunlight. This stops the plant from producing chlorophyll, which provides pigment, or color. To keep sunlight from reaching the spear, soil or hay is mounded over the first sign of shoots. Because white asparagus is more labor intensive and difficult to grow, it is usually more expensive than green asparagus.

ECKERT FAMILY FAVORITE
OVEN-ROASTED ASPARAGUS

2 lb. fresh asparagus spears, trimmed

2 Tbs. olive oil

½ tsp. Kosher salt

Preheat oven to 400 degrees. Place spears in a single layer on a rimmed sheet pan. Drizzle asparagus with oil and toss gently. Sprinkle with salt. Roast for 8-10 minutes or to desired doneness. (Roasting time will vary based on thickness of the spears.)

Herbs

Fresh herbs truly enhance recipes and really help pull it together. Sometimes you just need a hint of herbs for a delicate flavor, and other times handfuls are required.

Basil – one of the most important culinary herbs used in sauces, sandwiches, soups and salads. It is in top form when married with tomatoes;

Oregano – is similar to majoram, except more potent. It is great on salads, pizza and in tomato sauce;

Thyme – pairs well with other herbs, especially rosemary, parsley, sage or oregano. Its earthiness pairs with pork, lamb and duck;

Parsley – the workhorse of the herb world, can go in almost every dish. Flat-leaf parsley stands up better to heat so it is used in cooking, while curly parsley is used more decorative;

Mint – pairs perfectly with lamb, peas, carrots, tea, and drinks like mojitos and mint juleps;

Rosemary – has a pronounced lemon pine flavor that is strong, so it is used lightly. It compliments chicken, pork and olive oil.

FREEZING—Parsley, sage, rosemary, and thyme all freeze well. Pick them in the morning when the sun has brought up the herbs' essential oils. Wash, pat dry, and then strip the leaves from the stems. Place the leaves on a baking sheet lined with wax paper or baking parchment. Freeze for 4 hours, then place them in sealable, plastic freezer bags and seal tightly. Be certain to date and label the bags. Frozen herbs are best if used within 3 months.

KEEPING FRESH HERBS—Keep a small bouquet of fresh, stemmed herbs in a vase of fresh water on your kitchen counter while you are cooking. Not only does it brighten the kitchen, but it also fills your home with the satisfying scent of herbs. You may also wash and pat the herbs dry, wrap in a paper towel to absorb moisture, and then place in a sealable plastic bag and chill. The herbs should stay fresh for several days. Keep a glass of fresh herbs in the refrigerator, in place of the customary box of baking soda, to mask unpleasant odors.

Dry to fresh equivalent: 1 teaspoon dried herbs is equal to 1 tablespoon of fresh herbs. If a recipe calls for dry herbs, simply multiply the amount by 3 when using fresh herbs.

The Blooms & the Bees

Bloom is probably the most beautiful, picturesque time on the farm. The trees burst with color, signifying the hope of a great harvest. Apple trees have a more "showy" white bloom, while peach trees boast a pinkish bloom. The peach trees self-pollinate, but we must bring in bees to pollinate the apple trees. Truckloads of more than 125 bee hives, which look like rectangular boxes, arrive in the orchard in the middle of a spring night, and the bees begin their momentous 7- to 10-day task of pollinating thousands of trees planted on more than 100 acres of ground. An apple tree must be pollinated by an apple tree of a different variety, so we plant the apple orchards in alternating 4-row blocks of the same variety, or we use crabapples as a cross-pollinator within a large block of the same apple variety.

Spring is the time when we layout and plant new orchards. Preparation for planting starts three to four years before we plant the tree. In order to get the varieties and rootstocks that grow best in our climate, tree orders must be placed with nurseries three to four years ahead of planting. The ground where we plant is identified three years ahead of the planting, as well. We test the soil extensively for pH and nutrients and make the necessary adjustments. We then plant cover crops to help build organic matter and suppress invasive nematodes and weeds. Planting happens as soon as soil conditions allow in March. New orchards take three years to produce their first crop and 5 to 7 years to reach full production. Peaches stay in production for 15 to 18 years while apples stay in production for 22 to 25 years.

Sweet Snack

A bowl of cottage cheese topped with fresh sliced strawberries and drizzled with honey makes a perfect snack between meals.

Honey

The flavor, aroma, and color of honey vary greatly depending on the kind of flower from which the bees gather the nectar that is used to make the honey. Generally speaking, the lighter the honey, the milder the flavor.

WHEN SUBSTITUTING HONEY FOR SUGAR

1. Use equal amounts of honey for sugar up to 1 cup. For amounts greater than 1 cup, replace each cup of sugar with ⅔ to ¾ cup of honey.

2. Lower the baking temperature 25 degrees. Products with honey tend to brown faster.

3. In recipes using more than 1 cup of honey for sugar, it may be necessary to reduce liquids by ¼ cup per cup of honey.

4. In baked goods, add ¼ teaspoon of baking soda per cup of honey if baking soda is not already included in the recipe. This will reduce the acidity of the honey, as well as increase the volume of your product.

MEASURING—Honey can be measured easily by using the same cup used for the oil. Or coat the measuring cup or measuring spoon with non-stick pan coating spray.

GRANULATION—Most honey will naturally crystallize. To re-liquefy honey, place honey in its container into near boiling water that has been removed from heat. Stir as honey cools and turns clear. Honey can be melted in a microwave oven. Remove the container lid first.

QUICK HONEY IDEAS—Drizzle on aged cheddar cheese or blue cheese. Drizzle on hot oatmeal. Add to warm milk with cinnamon and nutmeg. Make an Elvis Presley sandwich with sliced bananas, peanut butter, and drizzled honey.

MOREL MUSHROOMS

Along with fruit trees blooming, we get pretty excited over "mushroom hunting season" in the spring. We won't give away our favorite hunting sites, but it is safe to say morel mushrooms grow well under apple trees. Mushroom hunting is a favorite activity for the entire Eckert family. Sometimes we hold contests to see who can find the most morels, and at the end of a great hunt, you can always rest assured there will be fried morels and egg morel scramble for everyone to enjoy.

BEETS

SELECTING—Choose beets that are small and firm with deep maroon coloring. Avoid beets that have a hairy taproot—this is usually an indication of age. Fresh beets should have the leaf stems still attached for ultimate freshness. Smaller beets will be sweeter and more tender.

STORING—Trim the leaves 2 inches from the root. Do not trim the tail. Place bulbs in a bag and store in a refrigerator for 7 to 10 days.

SPRING ONIONS & GARLIC

Spring onions are in fact very young onions, harvested in the spring. They have a milder flavor and therefore are delicious raw in salads, grilled or cooked. Often spring onions and scallions are referred to as green onions.

SPRING ONION—Has a bulb, usually sold in bunches of 2 to 3. Only available in spring.

SCALLION—Long and thin, with a straight bulb, usually sold in bunches of 5 to 6. Fresh with a mild flavor and cooks very quickly. Available year-round.

STORING—Both spring onions and scallions may be stored in a plastic bag in a refrigerator for up to 1 week.

GARLIC SELECTION & STORING—Choose garlic heads that are firm with no visible brown spots. Store unpeeled garlic heads in cool, dry place. Do not refrigerate. Properly stored, garlic can keep for up to 3 months. Aged garlic may produce green sprouts in the center of each clove. These are bitter, so discard them before chopping the garlic.

Strawberry Preserves

4 (8 oz.) canning jars
4 canning lids and rings
1½ quarts fresh strawberries, hulled
6 cups granulated sugar
½ cup bottled lemon juice

Wash jars in hot, soapy water. Rinse well. Place jars in a pan of hot boiling water. Reduce heat to simmer. Leave jars in hot water while preparing preserves. Place whole strawberries in a large kettle. Sprinkle granulated sugar over berries; cover and let stand at room temperature for 3 to 4 hours. Bring slowly to a boil, stirring occasionally until granulated sugar dissolves. Add lemon juice. Boil rapidly until thick, about 20 to 25 minutes. Stir frequently. Drain hot canning jars. Ladle immediately into hot canning jars; fill to ⅛ inch of top. With damp paper towel, wipe off rims. Screw on lids evenly and tightly, invert for a few seconds, and then stand up right to cool. Store in refrigerator and use within 4 weeks. Makes about 4 (8 oz.) jars.

—— *From Our Family Album* ——

The sixth generation fondly remembers
"strawberry preserves making day" on the farm. Grandma and Grandpa arrived early in the morning, and the children went out to the patch to pick the strawberries. They returned to the kitchen for stemming duty, while Grandma sterilized the jars and Mom stood at the stove constantly stirring strawberries, sugar and pectin. By the end of the day, many jars were filled and stored in the cellar to be shared throughout the year.

Honey Glaze for Chicken and Pork Kabobs

¼ cup vegetable oil

⅓ cup Eckert's Pure Honey

⅓ cup soy sauce

1 tsp. ground black pepper

2 cloves garlic, peeled

5 small Eckert's spring onions

2 red bell peppers cut in 2-inch pieces

8 skinless, boneless chicken breast halves, cut in 1-inch cubes *or* about 2 lbs. pork tenderloin, cut in 1-inch cubes

Skewers, soaked in water

In a large bowl, whisk together oil, honey, soy sauce, and pepper. Before adding chicken, reserve 4 tablespoons of marinade to brush onto kabobs while cooking. Place chicken, garlic, onions, and peppers in the bowl and marinate in the refrigerator 30 minutes to 2 hours.

Preheat grill to high. Drain marinade from the chicken and vegetables and discard marinade. Thread chicken or pork and vegetables alternately on the skewers.

Preheat grill for high heat. Clean and lightly oil grill grate. Place skewers on the grill. Cook for 12 to 15 minutes, or until chicken juices run clear, or the pork is slightly pink. Turn and brush with reserved marinade frequently.

Makes 8 to 10 servings.

SIDES

In the late 1970s, the Eckert family took a step back from the grocery store format and returned to their roots. They operated as a seasonal farm market with a variety of crops. The gambrel roof entry became an icon of Eckert's Country Store.

Asparagus & Morel Mushroom Stir-Fry

1 Tbs. vegetable oil

1 lb. asparagus, ends removed, cut into 1-inch diagonal slices

½ medium onion, sliced top to bottom

4 oz. sliced morel mushrooms (less if desired)

1 peeled garlic clove, crushed

1 Tbs. soy sauce

¼ cup chicken broth or water (or as needed)

1 Tbs. cornstarch dissolved in 1 Tbs. cold water

1 tsp. sesame oil (optional)

1 Tbs. toasted sesame seeds (optional)

Heat oil in wok or large frying pan. Add asparagus and stir-fry about 1 minute. Add onions and mushrooms. Stir-fry about 1 more minute. Add garlic, soy sauce, and small amount of chicken broth or water; cover. Simmer about 4 minutes or until asparagus is crisp-tender. Add sufficient cornstarch paste for desired consistency and heat until thick, about 2 to 3 minutes. Add sesame oil or sesame seeds if desired. Makes 4 servings.

NOTE: Add 4 to 6 ounces marinated ¼-inch thickness flank steak or chicken strips before asparagus. Stir-fry 2 to 3 minutes. Remove from wok; set aside. Add back into wok after sesame seeds.

Asparagus with Hollandaise Sauce

2 lbs. fresh whole asparagus spears, trimmed and blanched tender

½ cup unsalted butter

1 Tbs. white wine vinegar or fresh lemon juice

3 large egg yolks at room temperature

2 cups plus 4 Tbs. water

½ tsp. salt

⅛ tsp. cayenne pepper

In a small bowl or saucepan, melt butter and keep it warm. In another small bowl, warm vinegar or lemon juice (about 45 seconds in the microwave). In small saucepan, bring water to a boil. Place a small glass bowl on top of the saucepan making sure the water does not touch the bottom of the bowl. Place egg yolks in the bowl and beat with a wire whisk until they begin to thicken and are very creamy, about 4 minutes. Remove bowl from sauce pan. Separate and reserve 4 tablespoons of boiling water from the saucepan, then return yolk mixture in bowl to top of the saucepan. Add the water, 1 tablespoon at a time to the yolks, whisking after each addition. Add warm vinegar or lemon juice to yolk mixture while whisking. Remove yolk mixture from the saucepan. Whisk briskly while adding 1 tablespoon of butter at a time until fully incorporated. Add salt and cayenne pepper and whisk mixture until thickened, about 2 more minutes. Serve immediately over blanched asparagus.

NOTE: To blanch asparagus, bring a large pot of water and 1 tablespoon of salt to a boil. Add asparagus to water and boil for 2 to 4 minutes (thickness of stalks will vary boiling time) or until asparagus is bright green and crisp-tender. Place asparagus immediately in an ice water bath. Drain and blot asparagus dry with a clean towel.

Baked Asparagus with Walnuts and Gruyère Cheese

1 to 2 tsp. unsalted butter

1 lb. medium asparagus spears, trimmed and peeled

3 Tbs. water

½ cup grated Gruyère cheese

3 Tbs. English walnuts, chopped coarsely

1 Tbs. extra-virgin olive oil

Freshly ground black pepper to taste

Preheat oven to 350°F. Melt butter in a large oven-proof skillet on the stovetop over medium heat. Arrange asparagus in skillet, with the tips facing in one direction. Add three tablespoons water and cover skillet. Steam the asparagus for two minutes; remove skillet from the heat, and sprinkle cheese on asparagus. Sprinkle with walnuts and drizzle oil on top. Top with ground pepper. Place skillet in oven and bake uncovered, until the cheese has melted, about 5 minutes. Serve hot. Makes 4 servings.

—— *From Our Kitchen* ——

Crisp-tender is a term used to describe the doneness of vegetables cooked until they retain some of the crisp texture from their raw state.

Bundled Asparagus

4 slices Eckert's Farm Bread, crusts trimmed

16 medium stalks asparagus, trimmed

4 Tbs. "Quick Herb Spread" (see recipe on p. 30) or purchased garlic & herb cheese spread

1 to 2 Tbs. butter, melted

Preheat oven to 400°F. Blanch asparagus by dropping into boiling water for one minute. Then drain and cool with cold water to stop the cooking process. Drain well and set aside. Spread 1 tablespoon cheese on one side of each slice of bread. Lay 4 stalks of asparagus across bread from point to point. Roll other 2 points around asparagus and place "seam" side down on parchment paper lined baking sheet. Brush tops of bundles with melted butter and bake in oven until golden, about 7 minutes. Serve immediately. Makes 4 servings.

Roasted Asparagus with Feta

2½ lb. medium asparagus spears, trimmed

2 Tbs. olive oil

½ tsp. salt

¼ tsp. ground black pepper

¾ to 1 cup crumbled feta

Preheat oven to 500°F. Toss uncooked asparagus with oil, salt and pepper in a shallow oven-proof baking pan. Arrange asparagus in a single layer. Place pan in oven. Bake 10 to 14 minutes or until lightly browned and fork tender. About half way through roasting, top asparagus with feta. Makes 5 to 6 servings.

White Asparagus with Cream Sauce and Parmesan

8 to 10 white asparagus spears
(medium thickness)

1 tsp. cornstarch

1 tsp. cold water

½ cup reserved asparagus liquid
(see instructions)

½ cup heavy cream

About ½ cup Parmesan cheese,
grated

Preheat oven to 200°F. Peel white asparagus and remove the tough ends. Reserve peelings and ends. In a large skillet, add enough boiling water to cover the peeling and ends as well as trimmed asparagus spears. (Do not add more boiling water than needed to cover asparagus.) Return water to a boil and simmer covered until the spears are fork-tender, about 15 minutes. Remove asparagus spears, pat dry. Reserve asparagus cooking water, peels and ends. Place spears in an oven-proof dish. Place in preheated oven to keep warm. Using the cooking water with the peels and ends, bring back to a boil and reduce the liquid in the skillet to ½ cup, about 10 to 12 minutes. Strain liquid and discard the peels and ends. Return liquid to skillet. In a small bowl, mix cornstarch with 1 teaspoon cold water until smooth. Whisk cornstarch mixture into asparagus liquid. Then whisk in heavy cream. Bring to a boil and immediately reduce heat to simmer. Cook stirring continually until the liquid turns clear and is slightly thick, about 2 to 3 minutes. (Do not boil.) Turn off heat. Remove asparagus spears from oven. Spoon cream sauce over spears. Top with Parmesan cheese and serve immediately. Makes 2 to 3 servings.

Oven-Baked White Asparagus

1 lb. white asparagus spears, ends
trimmed and peeled
2 Tbs. butter
Salt and pepper

Preheat oven at 350°F. Wash asparagus and place spears on a large sheet of heavy-duty aluminum foil; dot with butter. Bring edges of foil together to form a pouch, seal tightly and place on a cookie sheet. Bake for 25 to 30 minutes or until asparagus is "crisp-tender." Carefully open foil to allow steam to escape. Season with salt and pepper to taste. Makes 4 servings.

Asparagus and Morel Mushrooms with Linguine

1 lb. green asparagus, cut into
1-inch pieces
1 pkg. (16 oz.) uncooked linguine
1 to 2 cups reserved hot pasta water
¼ cup pine nuts or walnuts
3 Tbs. butter
2 cups Morel mushrooms, sliced in
half, lengthwise
2 Tbs. finely chopped green onions
1 cup whipping cream or half and
half
Salt and pepper
½ cup grated Parmesan cheese

Steam asparagus until fork tender. Bring a large pot of salted water to boil; cook linguine according to package directions. Drain pasta reserving 1 to 2 cups pasta water and set both aside. Meanwhile, in a heavy frying pan, toast nuts over medium heat until lightly browned and fragrant, about 2 to 3 minutes. Remove from pan and set aside. Melt butter in frying pan, then add mushrooms and onions. Cook, stirring often, until mushrooms are lightly browned and onions begin to look translucent, about 5 minutes. Add cream to pan and bring mixture to a low boil, stirring constantly. Reduce heat and cook until mixture begins to thicken. Bring reserved pasta water to a boil. Pour over pasta to reheat. Drain pasta. Place linguine in a large serving bowl. Add asparagus to sauce and season with salt and pepper to taste. Spoon sauce over linguine and top with Parmesan cheese. Makes 4 to 6 servings.

Farfalle with Asparagus and Mushrooms

Salt

1 lb. uncooked farfalle pasta

1 cup reserved hot pasta water

3 Tbs. unsalted butter

1 lb. cremini mushrooms or morel mushrooms, trimmed and thickly sliced

1 lb. thin asparagus, trimmed and cut crosswise into 1-inch pieces

1 cup mascarpone cheese

Pinch of freshly grated nutmeg

¾ cup toasted walnuts, coarsely chopped, divided

Freshly ground black pepper

¼ to ½ cup freshly grated Parmesan cheese

Bring a large pot of salted water to boil. Add the farfalle and cook. Stir often to prevent the pasta from sticking together, until tender but still firm to the bite, about 12 minutes. Drain, reserving 1 cup of the hot pasta liquid. Meanwhile, melt the butter in a large, heavy skillet over medium heat. Add the mushrooms and sauté until they are tender and most of their juices have evaporated, about 5 minutes. Add the asparagus and sauté until it is crisp-tender, about 5 minutes. Stir in the mascarpone and nutmeg. Add the cooked farfalle and toss until the cheese coats the pasta, adding the reserved cooking liquid ¼ cup at a time to moisten. Stir in ½ cup of the walnuts. Season the pasta to taste with salt and pepper. Mound the pasta in a large, wide serving bowl. Sprinkle with the Parmesan cheese and remaining ¼ cup of walnuts and serve. Makes 4 servings.

Roasted Beets with Feta

4 medium beets, peeled and cut into ½-inch pieces

1 Tbs. olive oil

1 tsp. salt

Pepper to taste

4 scallions, chopped

2 tsp. lemon juice

⅓ cup crumbled feta

Preheat oven to 450°F. Toss beets with olive oil, salt and pepper on baking sheet. Roast in oven, for about 35 minutes or until tender, turning beets once halfway through roasting. Transfer to bowl and toss with scallions and lemon juice. Top with crumbled feta. Makes 2 servings.

Green Beans with Basil and Mint

1 to 1½ lbs. green beans, stem ends trimmed

2 tsp. salt

⅓ cup fresh basil leaves, coarsely chopped or torn

¼ cup fresh mint leaves, coarsely chopped or torn

2 Tbs. olive oil

1 clove of garlic, minced fine

Salt and ground pepper to taste

Heat a large pot of water to boiling. Add the green beans and salt. Return to a boil and cook green beans until tender but still bright green, about 8 minutes. Drain immediately. In a serving bowl, combine basil, mint, oil, and garlic. Place green beans in bowl and toss. Season as desired with salt and pepper. Serve warm or at room temperature. Makes 4 servings.

Risotto with Spring Vegetables

8 oz. asparagus spears, ends trimmed and spears cut into 2-inch pieces

3 Tbs. olive oil, divided

4 cups chicken stock

¾ cup finely chopped shallots

½ cup chopped carrots

1 cup uncooked Arborio rice or other medium-grain rice

2 cups frozen green peas, thawed

½ cup dry white wine

¾ cup grated fresh Parmesan cheese

¼ cup finely chopped fresh parsley

Salt and freshly ground black pepper

Preheat oven to 400°F. Toss asparagus with 1 tablespoon olive oil and roast for 5 to 8 minutes or until asparagus is fork tender; set aside. Bring chicken stock to a gentle simmer in a saucepan. Keep warm over low heat. Heat 2 tablespoons oil in a large Dutch oven or heavy bottomed pot over medium-high heat. Add shallots and carrots to Dutch oven and cook 4 to 5 minutes, stirring occasionally. Add rice and cook 2 to 3 minutes, stirring frequently. Add wine and stir until the liquid is completely absorbed, 3 to 4 minutes. Add 1 cup stock; cook 4 to 5 minutes or until liquid is nearly absorbed, stirring constantly. Add remaining stock, ½ cup at a time, stirring frequently until each portion of stock is absorbed before adding the next (about 30 minutes total). Stir in peas and asparagus with last addition of stock. Remove from heat; stir in cheese and parsley. Adjust seasoning as desired with salt and pepper. Makes 6 servings.

Asparagus-New Potato Hash

1 lb. small unpeeled red potatoes
2 shallots, minced
2 Tbs. olive oil
1 lb. fresh asparagus, ends removed, cut into ½-inch pieces
1 tsp. chopped fresh thyme
1 tsp. salt
½ tsp. pepper
2 tsp. fresh lemon juice
½ cup grated cheddar cheese
Lemon slices for garnish

In a Dutch oven, add potatoes and enough salted water to cover. Bring to a boil over medium-high heat. Cook 15 minutes or just until tender; drain well. Cool 15 minutes; cut potatoes into quarters. In a large non-stick skillet, sauté shallots in oil over medium heat for 1 minute. Add asparagus, thyme, salt, pepper and lemon juice. Sauté 2 to 3 minutes or until asparagus is crisp-tender. Add potatoes and sauté 3 more minutes or until mixture is thoroughly heated. Remove from heat and sprinkle with cheese. Garnish with lemon slices. Makes 8 servings.

Potluck Cheesy Corn

2½ lbs. Eckert's frozen yellow corn
2 Tbs. granulated sugar
3 Tbs. water
3 Tbs. milk
4 Tbs. butter
8 oz. cream cheese, cubed
6 slices (about 6 oz.) yellow or white American cheese

Place corn in a slow cooker. Add sugar, water, milk and butter to corn. Top ingredients with cream cheese cubes and cheese slices. Ingredients will blend as the corn cooks. Set slow cooker on low. Cook about 3½ to 4 hours, stirring occasionally. Makes 10 to 12 servings.

Potato Salad
with Garlic Scapes, Peas and Green Onions

3 lbs. small to medium unpeeled yukon gold potatoes

Kosher salt

¼ lb. garlic scapes, pods and tips removed

1½ cups peas

½ cup mayonnaise

¼ cup extra-virgin olive oil

1 large lemon, finely grated to yield 2 tsp. zest

2 Tbs. fresh lemon juice

Freshly ground black pepper

2 Tbs. rice vinegar

½ cup thinly sliced green onions or scallions

⅓ cup chopped fresh flat-leaf parsley

½ cup chopped fresh mint

Put the potatoes in a 6-quart pot; add 2 tablespoons salt and enough water to cover by 1 inch. Put the scapes on the potatoes. Bring to a boil over high heat, then lower the heat to medium. Simmer vigorously until the scapes are just tender, about 5 minutes after the water boils. With tongs, transfer the scapes to a cutting board and cut into ½-inch pieces. Continue to simmer the potatoes until just tender when pierced with a fork, about 15 minutes longer. Add the peas and simmer until crisp-tender, 1 to 2 minutes. Drain the potatoes and peas in a colander. With tongs, transfer the potatoes to a cutting board. Rinse the peas under cold water to stop the cooking process, and let drain. While the potatoes cool, whisk the mayonnaise, oil, lemon zest and juice and ½ teaspoon each salt and pepper in a small bowl. In a large bowl, mix the vinegar with 2 teaspoons salt and stir to dissolve. When the potatoes are just cool enough to handle, scrape their skins off with a paring knife and cut them into ¾ to 1-inch pieces. Toss them in the vinegar-salt mixture, and then stir in about half of the dressing. Add the scapes, peas, green onions, herbs, the remaining dressing and salt and pepper to taste. Mix well. Let cool to room temperature before serving. Makes 6 to 8 servings.

Amish Noodles with Spinach and Ham

2 lbs. fresh spinach
6 oz. Amish wide noodles
3 Tbs. butter
½ cup chopped spring onions or yellow onion
1 garlic clove, minced
½ cup diced ham
3 Tbs. flour
2½ cups cream or light cream
½ tsp. salt
¼ cup fresh grated Parmesan cheese

Preheat oven to 400°F. Wash and trim spinach. Place the spinach in a large pan over medium heat. Stir 2 to 3 minutes or until the spinach is wilted. Drain and squeeze dry, then chop. Cook the noodles according to the package directions and drain. Melt butter in a large saucepan over medium heat. Add onions and sauté until transparent, 4 to 5 minutes. Add the garlic and ham. Sauté for 3 minutes while stirring. Lower the heat and stir in the flour until well blended, 1 to 2 minutes. Add the cream and continue to stir. Remove pan from heat and stir in noodles and spinach. Salt to taste. Pour into a 9 × 11 inch pan, sprinkle with cheese and bake for 15 minutes or until cheese is melted. Makes 8 servings.

Cheddar Bacon Deviled Eggs

12 hard-cooked eggs (see recipe on p. 48)
½ cup mayonnaise
1 cup sour cream
½ tsp. Dijon mustard
1 tsp. fresh lemon juice
¼ tsp. pepper
½ cup crumbled cooked Eckert's bacon
¼ cup finely shredded cheddar cheese
2 Tbs. green onions

Cut eggs in half lengthwise. Remove and place yolks in a medium bowl. Mash yolks with a fork. Stir in mayonnaise, sour cream, mustard, lemon juice, and pepper. Mix well before adding bacon, cheese and onions. Stir until well combined. Spoon about 1 tablespoon of yolk mixture into each egg white half. Cover and refrigerate before serving. Makes 24.

Perfect Hard-Cooked Eggs

Uncooked eggs | Place eggs in saucepan large enough to hold them in a single layer. Add cold water to cover the eggs by 1 inch. Heat saucepan over high heat to just boiling. Remove from heat and cover. Let eggs stand in hot water for about 15 minutes. Gently remove eggs from water and serve warm, or cool completely under running water or in a bowl of ice water. Refrigerate when cooled.

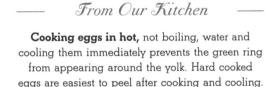

From Our Kitchen

Cooking eggs in hot, not boiling, water and cooling them immediately prevents the green ring from appearing around the yolk. Hard cooked eggs are easiest to peel after cooking and cooling.

Entrées

— From Our Family Album —

To mark the 100-year anniversary of retail and to recommit to their guests and community, the Eckert family built a new store just to the north of the original store in 2010. The Eckert family proudly operates in this space today.

Easter Honey Glazed Ham

10 to 12 lb. fully cooked, bone-in ham
⅓ cup Eckert's Pure Honey
1 cup brown sugar
⅓ cup pineapple juice
⅓ cup orange juice
2 Tbs. Dijon mustard
¼ tsp. ground cloves

Preheat oven to 325°F. Place ham in roasting pan. Bake uncovered 2 hours. In a small saucepan, combine honey, brown sugar, pineapple and orange juice, mustard and cloves. Bring to a boil; reduce heat and simmer for 5 to 10 minutes. Set aside.

After baking the ham brush ham with glaze and bake an additional 30 to 45 minutes, brushing on glaze every 10 minutes. Makes 15 servings.

Baked Crab Cakes

16 oz. lump crab meat
1 large egg
1 large egg white
1 medium green bell pepper, finely minced
1 medium yellow bell pepper, finely minced
1 medium red bell pepper, finely minced
¾ cup real mayonnaise (not light)
1½ cups panko bread crumbs
3 tsp. Old Bay® seasoning
½ tsp. kosher salt
¼ tsp. fresh ground pepper
½ medium lemon, squeezed
½ tsp. lemon zest

Preheat oven to 425°F. Check over crab meat for any shell pieces; remove and set crab meat aside. In a medium bowl, whisk eggs together. By hand, stir crab and remaining ingredients gently until well mixed. Coat the inside of a ¼ cup measuring cup with cooking spray or vegetable oil. Use the measuring cup to form 18 to 20 cakes, recoating the cup as needed to prevent mixture from sticking. Gently press each cake to 1 inch thickness on a foiled or parchment lined baking pan. Bake 15 to 20 minutes or until golden brown. The crab cakes do not need to be turned. Makes about 18 to 20 crab cakes.

Family Breakfast Strata

4 oz. fresh or defrosted sliced mushrooms, divided

2 Tbs. butter, divided

14 to 18 Eckert's Country White bread slices, crusts removed, divided

12 oz. Eckert's uncooked diced thick sliced bacon, divided

3¾ cups milk

8 large eggs, lightly beaten

½ tsp. salt

½ lb. grated cheddar cheese, divided

½ lb. grated Swiss cheese, divided

In a small skillet sauté mushrooms in 1 tablespoon butter for 2 to 3 minutes. Grease bottom and sides of a 9 × 13 inch baking dish with remaining 1 tablespoon of butter. Line dish with ½ of the bread slices. Over top of bread, layer ½ of the diced bacon, cheddar and Swiss cheese. Set aside. In a large bowl, mix milk, eggs and salt together. Pour ½ of the milk-egg mixture over the bread and cheese. Layer the remaining bread slices, bacon, and cheese. Pour remaining milk-egg mixture over the top. Cover and refrigerate overnight. Preheat oven to 325°F when ready to bake. Bake uncovered 50 to 60 minutes or until golden brown on top. Cover with foil the last 15 minutes if browning too quickly. Allow to set 15 minutes before cutting and serving.

Makes 8 servings.

NOTE: We recommend serving this strata with Eckert's Homemade Tomato Salsa.

Chicken & Asparagus
with Melted Gruyère Cheese

8 oz. asparagus, trimmed and cut into 1-inch pieces, about 2 cups

⅔ cup chicken broth

2 tsp. plus ¼ cup flour, divided

4 boneless, skinless chicken breasts (about 1 to 1¼ lbs.), trimmed

¼ tsp. salt

½ tsp. freshly ground pepper

1 to 2 Tbs. canola oil

1 shallot, thinly sliced

½ cup dry white wine

⅓ cup dairy sour cream

1 Tbs. chopped fresh tarragon or 1 tsp. dried

2 tsp. lemon juice

⅓ to ½ cup shredded Gruyère cheese

Place a steamer basket in a large saucepan, add 1 inch of water and bring to boil. Add asparagus; cover and steam for 3 minutes. Uncover, remove asparagus and set aside. Whisk broth and 2 teaspoons flour in a small bowl until smooth. Set aside. Place the remaining ¼ cup flour in a shallow dish. Sprinkle chicken with salt and pepper and dredge both sides in the flour, shaking off any excess. Heat oil in a large skillet over medium heat. Add the chicken and cook until golden brown, 3 to 4 minutes per side, adjusting heat as needed to prevent scorching. Transfer to a plate and cover to keep warm. Add shallot, wine and reserved broth mixture to pan; cook over medium heat, stirring, until thickened, about 2 minutes. Reduce heat to medium-low; stir in sour cream, tarragon, lemon juice, and steamed asparagus. Mix gently until combined. Return the chicken to the pan and turn to coat with sauce. Sprinkle cheese on top of each piece of chicken, cover and continue cooking until the cheese is melted, about 2 minutes. Makes 4 servings.

From Our Kitchen

If you don't have white wine handy, you can substitute chicken broth or dry vermouth.

Chicken Breasts with Garlic Herb Butter

1 head garlic

1 to 2 Tbs. olive oil

3 Tbs. fresh thyme, chopped

3 Tbs. fresh rosemary, chopped

3 Tbs. fresh sage, chopped

3 Tbs. fresh parsley, chopped

1 cup unsalted butter, room
temperature, divided

3 tsp. kosher salt

4 bone-in, skin-on chicken breasts

Preheat oven to 400°F. With a knife, trim the papery tip off the head of garlic to expose the white tips of the cloves (remove about ¼ to ½ inch of the tip end). Leave cloves connected to the root end. Place bulb of cloves on aluminum foil. Drizzle with oil and wrap with foil. Bake for 30 to 45 minutes, or until cloves are soft when pressed. Remove foil and allow bulb to cool. Using a small knife, cut the skin slightly around each clove and extract the soft garlic from the skin and discard skin. In a small bowl, combine herbs, butter and garlic. Mix until smooth. Rinse chicken breasts with water; pat dry. Reserve ⅓ of butter mixture to coat chicken skin. Gently separate skin from chicken breasts, place butter mixture between chicken skin and flesh. Coat exterior with butter mixture. Roast until skin begins to brown, about 5 minutes. Reduce oven temperature to 375°F for about 30 to 40 minutes or until the chicken reaches an internal temperature of 165°F. Remove from oven and let stand for 5 minutes before serving. Makes 4 servings.

--- *From Our Kitchen* ---

If you are short on fresh herbs, don't hesitate to substitute dried herbs. Three tablespoons of fresh herbs are equivalent to 3 teaspoons of dried herbs. We recommend experimenting with your favorite herbs to make your seasoning combinations unique.

Grilled Pork Steaks with Vidalia Onion BBQ Sauce

2 1-inch thick cut pork steaks, brined (see recipe on p. 55)

1 to 2 Tbs. olive oil

Salt and pepper

½ to ¾ cup Eckert's Vidalia Onion BBQ Sauce

Brine pork steaks 1 to 2 hours. Remove from brine and pat dry. Preheat grill. Clean and oil grates. Drizzle olive oil over the pork steak and rub with salt and pepper. Turn steak over and repeat on other side. Slow cook the pork steaks on indirect heat for 30 to 40 minutes (until internal temperature of 135°F is reached). Move pork steak to direct heat to finish cooking to internal temperature of 145°F while basting with Vidalia BBQ Sauce. Makes 2 servings.

Shrimp, Poultry or Pork Brine

½ cup kosher salt
½ cup granulated sugar
2 cups hot water (not boiling)

Combine ingredients. Stir to dissolve salt and sugar. Add 2 to 3 cups crushed ice; stir until cool. Pour brine into a large food-grade plastic bag, stainless steel or glass container. Add food; cover and refrigerate following the brining chart below. Recipe may be increased as needed to cover the food being brined. When ready to cook, remove meat from brine; pat dry with paper towels. Discard brine. Proceed with your recipe. Makes about 4 cups.

BRINING TIME:
Shrimp: 30 minutes
Chicken Breasts: 1 hour
Whole Chicken: 1½ hours
Whole Turkey: 6 to 12 hours
Pork Chops (bone-in or boneless): 2 hours

—— *From Our Kitchen* ——

Brining allows the meat muscle strands to relax and the brine to enter the cells. This adds moisture and tenderness, creating a juicy cooked product. Marinades add flavor, but do not tenderize as much as brine.

Steak with Fresh-Herb Chimichurri

MARINADE FOR STEAK

1 tsp. minced garlic

1 tsp. chopped fresh cilantro

4 Tbs. olive oil

3 Tbs. agave syrup

1 Tbs. fresh lemon juice

1 Tbs. fresh lime juice

½ tsp. kosher salt

1 tsp. freshly ground black pepper

1½ to 2 lbs. flank steak, trimmed

HERB CHIMICHURRI

2 Tbs. fresh chopped cilantro

2 Tbs. fresh chopped flat-leaf parsley

1 Tbs. fresh chopped basil

1 Tbs. fresh chopped oregano

3 Tbs. chopped onion

3 Tbs. chopped red bell pepper

3 Tbs. chopped green bell pepper

4 large garlic cloves, peeled and smashed

1 tsp. kosher salt

1 Tbs. freshly ground black pepper

½ tsp. ground cumin

2 Tbs. rice vinegar

2 Tbs. fresh lime juice

1 to 2 tsp. red chili flakes

¼ cup olive oil

Combine marinade ingredients in a large glass bowl. Add flank steak. Cover and marinate in the refrigerator for 1 to 3 hours.

TO PREPARE CHIMICHURRI SAUCE: Pulse all ingredients in a food processor until a coarse sauce forms. Cover and set aside for 2 hours in the refrigerator.

Preheat grill to high or heat a large heavy bottom skillet over high heat. Drain the marinade from steaks and discard marinade. Cook steak to medium-rare, 4 to 6 minutes on each side. Let steak sit for 5 to 10 minutes, then cut against the grain into ¼-inch slices and top with Chimichurri Sauce. Makes 4 servings.

Strawberry, Grilled Turkey, and Goat Cheese Panini

1 (4 oz.) goat cheese log, softened
8 Italian bread slices
8 oz. thinly sliced smoked turkey
8 fresh basil leaves
½ to ¾ cup sliced fresh strawberries
2 Tbs. Eckert's red pepper jelly
2 Tbs. butter, melted
4 strawberry halves, for garnish

Cut goat cheese into 4 even portions. Divide turkey, basil leaves, strawberries and goat cheese evenly among 4 bread slices. Spread 1½ teaspoons pepper jelly on 1 side of remaining bread slices; place bread slices, jelly side down, on top of goat cheese. Brush sandwiches with melted butter. Grill in pan 2 minutes per side. Garnish. Makes 4 servings.

—— *From Our Family Album* ——

Years ago we used helicopters and pilots from local television stations to help us protect apple blooms from dangerously cold temperatures in the spring. The pilots watched temperatures with us until they approached 28 degrees. Then helicopters were sent to the orchards to mix warm and cold layers of air in hopes of raising the temperature near the blooms.

Eckert's Porterhouse Steak with Andria's Steak Sauce

1½ to 1¾ inch thick Eckert's
Porterhouse Steak
½ Tbs. canola oil
Kosher salt
Fresh cracked pepper
2 Tbs. Andria's Steak Sauce

Remove steak from the refrigerator and coat with kosher salt. Allow steak to warm at room temperature for at least 45 minutes. Before grilling, rub steak with canola oil and season with kosher salt and fresh cracked pepper. Grill steak at high heat on lower rack for 2 minutes, turn steak 90 degrees and grill for an additional 2 minutes. Flip the steak and repeat to create char marks. Move steak to upper rack and turn grill to medium heat. While the steak is on the upper rack, flip and apply Andria's steak sauce every 2 to 3 minutes. Cook steak to your desired internal temperature. Total cooking time for medium/medium rare steak is 20 to 30 minutes.

From Our Kitchen

Eckert's purchases steers from a local farmer and they are processed locally. Eckert's skilled butchers cut the steaks for the meat case daily. Porterhouse steaks are a family favorite in the summer. Grilling them often results in extra guests at the dinner table!

Oven-Baked Bacon

¾ to 1 lb. Eckert's bacon

Place oven rack in middle position. Preheat oven to 375°F. Line a rimmed baking sheet with parchment paper or aluminum foil. Place strips of bacon in rows without touching. Bake 15 to 20 minutes or until the desired crispness. Transfer bacon to paper towel-lined plate; blot dry. To serve later, wrap bacon in paper towels and place in an air-tight container or plastic bag; refrigerate until ready to serve. Bacon can be baked 3 to 4 days ahead of time. Reheat in microwave for 5 to 10 seconds just before serving.

Linguine and Prosciutto Frittatas

½ lb. linguine
7 large eggs
½ cup milk
¼ cup heavy cream
½ cup mascarpone cheese
6 oz. diced prosciutto
5 oz. mozzarella cheese, diced (1 cup diced) or smoked mozzarella
½ cup freshly grated Asiago cheese
¼ cup finely chopped fresh flat-leaf parsley
2 garlic cloves, minced
1 tsp. salt
¾ freshly ground black pepper
⅛ tsp. freshly grated nutmeg

Bring a large pot of salted water to a boil over high heat. Add the pasta and cook until tender, 8 to 10 minutes. Drain the pasta. Use kitchen shears to cut the linguine into smaller pieces. The pasta should measure about 3 cups. Preheat the oven to 350°F. Grease a 12 cup muffin tin. In a blender, combine the eggs, milk, cream and mascarpone. Blend until well combined. Transfer the mixture to a large bowl and add the cut pasta, prosciutto, mozzarella, Asiago, parsley, garlic salt, pepper, and nutmeg. Stir until the ingredients are combined. Fill each of the muffin cups to top. Bake until firm and cooked through, 30 to 35 minutes. Let the frittatas cool for 3 minutes before removing from tin. Makes 6 servings.

Grilled Fresh Eckert's Sausage with Spring Onions

4 to 5 small to medium Eckert's spring onions, halved and cut into ¼-inch thick slices

1 to 2 tsp. fresh thyme leaves

Kosher salt

Freshly ground black pepper

2 lbs. fresh Eckert's sausages (about 8 links)

8 Eckert's bakery buns

On a gas grill, turn burners to medium-high with lid closed. Heat grill until very hot, about 10 minutes. Scrape grate clean before starting to grill. Meanwhile, combine onion, thyme, salt and pepper to taste, in medium microwave-safe bowl. Cover with plastic wrap and microwave on high power about 2 to 3 minutes or until onions begin to soften, stirring after 1 minute. Transfer onions to disposable aluminum roasting pan. Place sausages in single layer over onions. Tightly cover roasting pan with foil. Place roasting pan in center of grill, cook about 15 minutes. Move pan to one side of grill and with caution, remove the foil cover releasing the steam toward the back of the grill. Use tongs and place sausages directly on grate. Grill sausages uncovered until golden brown on all sides, about 5 to 6 minutes. Turn sausages to help with the browning. Transfer sausages to a platter; cover loosely with foil. Continue cooking the onions until onions begin to brown, about 5 to 6 minutes. Serve sausage on bun topped with onions. Makes 4 to 8 servings.

—— *From Our Kitchen* ——

Eckert's butchers make fresh sausage daily in our Meat Department inside the Country Store. Our applewurst sausage, made with local pork and chunks of apple, is a year-round customer favorite!

Steak Hoagies
with Eckert's Spring Onions and Cheese

2 strip steaks, about 1-inch thick

Kosher salt and black pepper

2 to 3 Tbs. vegetable oil

2 Eckert's spring onions, sliced thin

1 green bell pepper, seeded, sliced thin

8 oz. button mushrooms, sliced thin

2 to 3 Tbs. Eckert's Vidalia Onion Steak Sauce

1 to 2 Tbs. fresh oregano leaves or ½ to 2 tsp. dried oregano

4 Eckert's sub rolls slit partially open lengthwise

6 oz. thinly sliced provolone cheese

Adjust oven rack to upper middle position and preheat oven to 400°F. Allow steaks to stand at room temperature at least 45 minutes. Pat steak dry with paper towels and season with salt and pepper. Heat 1 to 2 tablespoons oil in large stainless steel skillet over medium heat until the oil is just smoking. Cook steaks until well-browned, about 3 to 5 minutes per side. Transfer to plate and allow to rest about 5 minutes, then slice thin against the grain. In the same skillet, add remaining oil, onion, bell pepper, mushrooms and ½ teaspoon salt. Cook vegetables about 8 to 10 minutes or until tender but still crisp. Remove from heat. Add in steak sauce, oregano and sliced steak to the cooked vegetable mixture. Gently combine. Divide steak mixture among rolls and top with cheese. Arrange sandwiches on rimmed baking pan and bake until cheese is melted, about 3 to 5 minutes. Makes 4 servings.

Marinated Kabobs

MARINADE

½ to ¾ cup olive oil

6 small garlic cloves, peeled and minced (about 2 Tbs.)

¼ cup minced fresh cilantro or minced mint leaves

1 to 2 tsp mixed dried Italian herbs

1 tsp. salt

Ground black pepper

MEAT

1½ lbs. boneless, skinless chicken breasts or thighs, pork or beef, cut into 1 to 1½-inch pieces

VEGETABLES

3 cups of mixed vegetables (½-inch zucchini rounds; chunks of red or green bell pepper; onion wedges; whole medium mushrooms; large peeled garlic cloves)

2 to 3 Tbs. olive oil to coat vegetables

Kosher salt & freshly cracked black pepper

8 bamboo skewers, soaked in water

Whisk all marinade ingredients in small bowl. Mix marinade and chicken, pork, or beef in gallon-size zipper-lock plastic bag; seal bag and refrigerate, turning once or twice, until meat has marinated, at least 30 minutes, up to 2 hours. Preheat grill to medium-low. Meanwhile, lightly coat vegetables by tossing in medium bowl with oil, salt and pepper to taste. Remove meat pieces from bag; discard marinade. Thread meat and vegetables alternately onto skewers. Grill, turning each kabob one quarter turn every 2 minutes, until meat and vegetables are lightly browned and meat is fully cooked, about 8 to 10 minutes. Check for doneness by cutting into one of the meat pieces. Remove kabobs from grill. Serve immediately. Makes 8 kabobs (4 servings).

From Our Kitchen

Although white breast meat can be used, we prefer the juicier, more flavorful dark thigh meat for these kabobs. Whichever you choose, do not mix white and dark meat on the same skewer, since they cook at slightly different rates. Double skewering makes for easier turning on the grill. Use one hand to hold two skewers about ½-inch apart, then thread the chicken, meat and vegetables on both skewers at once.

Lana's Mini Quiche

3 large eggs
½ cup heavy cream
½ to ¾ cup whole milk
1 tsp. fresh chopped parsley, flat or curly leaf, optional
4 to 6 dashes Tabasco or other hot sauce
Loaf of Eckert's Hummingbird Bread

Preheat oven to 325°F. Spray 12-cup muffin tin with non-stick spray. Cut crust off bread (save for later use). Roll bread flat with a rolling pin. Trim bread to fit the mini quiche dish/pan as needed. In a medium bowl, mix eggs, cream, milk, parsley and hot sauce until combined. Pour egg mixture into a 2 quart pitcher for easy filling. Fill cups with egg mixture. Bake 15 to 20 minutes or until golden brown on top. Check for doneness by sticking a thin knife tip into the custard; the knife should come out clean. Serve with Eckert's salsa or guacamole. Makes about 1½ dozen.

— *From Our Kitchen* —

Curly leaf and Italian or flat-leaf parsley can both be used in cooking. However, we prefer the flavor of flat-leaf parsley. Curly leaf parsley makes a lovely garnish for plates and it does just fine in a culinary pinch.

Delicious add-ins include ¼ cup uncooked chopped broccoli florets, ¼ cup crumbled blue cheese, 2 to 3 slices cooked crumbled bacon. Mix all together in a 2-quart bowl.

Chicken with 40 Roasted Garlic Cloves

1 whole chicken (3-½ to 4 lbs.), cut into 8 pieces, skin on

Ground black pepper

Kosher salt

3 to 4 large heads garlic, outer papery skins removed, cloves separated and unpeeled (reserve 10 roasted cloves to use later in sauce)

4 to 5 Eckert's spring onions, peeled and cut into quarters

3 Tbs. vegetable oil, divided

2 sprigs fresh thyme

1 sprig fresh rosemary

1 bay leaf

¾ cup dry vermouth or dry white wine

¾ cup low-sodium chicken broth

2 Tbs. unsalted butter

Cover chicken pieces in brine and refrigerate until fully seasoned, about 30 minutes but not more than 2 hours. (See page 55 for brining instructions.) Rinse chicken pieces under running water and thoroughly pat dry with paper towels. Season both sides of chicken pieces with pepper. Adjust oven rack to middle position and preheat oven to 400°F. Next, toss 40 unpeeled garlic cloves and quartered spring onions with 2 tablespoons vegetable oil, salt and pepper in a 2-quart oven-proof baking dish. Cover tightly with foil and roast until softened and beginning to brown, about 30 minutes, shaking pan once to toss contents after 15 minutes. Uncover, stir, and continue to roast until browned and fully tender, about 10 minutes longer, stirring once or twice. Remove from oven; set aside to cool slightly, about 10 minutes. Meanwhile, increase oven temperature to 450°F. Using kitchen string, tie together thyme, rosemary and bay leaf; set aside. Heat remaining 1 tablespoon oil in 12-inch heavy-bottomed ovenproof skillet over medium-high heat until oil begins to smoke. Brown chicken pieces skin-side down until deep golden, about 5 minutes. Using tongs, turn chicken pieces and brown until golden on second side, about 4 minutes longer. Turn off heat. Transfer chicken to large plate. Discard fat but leave chicken drippings. Add vermouth, chicken broth and tied herb bundle, scraping bottom of skillet with wooden spoon to loosen browned bits. Squeeze roasted garlic out of each garlic skin into a small bowl. Discard garlic skins. Reserve 10 to 12 cooked cloves; set aside. Set skillet over medium heat, add remaining peeled garlic/onion mixture to pan and browned chicken, skin-side up, to skillet. Place skillet in oven and roast about 10 to 12 minutes or until instant-read thermometer inserted into thickest part of breast registers about 165°F. If desired, increase heat to broil and broil to crisp skin, 3 to 5 minutes. Remove skillet from oven and transfer chicken to serving dish. Scatter remaining garlic cloves around chicken and discard herbs. Reserve juices and drippings left in skillet. With spatula, scrape reserved drippings and simmer over medium-high heat, whisking occasionally to incorporate garlic; adjust seasoning with salt and pepper to taste. Whisk in butter; pour sauce into sauceboat and serve over chicken pieces. Makes 4 servings.

Eckert's Sunday Family Garlic Beef Roast

ROAST

8 large cloves garlic, unpeeled

1 top boneless sirloin roast (4 lbs.), with some fat intact

RUB

3 large cloves garlic, peeled and minced

1 tsp. dried thyme

½ tsp salt

GARLIC PASTE

12 large cloves garlic, peeled, cloves cut in half lengthwise

2 sprigs fresh thyme

2 bay leaves

½ tsp. salt

½ cup olive oil

Ground black pepper

AU JUS SAUCE

1½ cups low-sodium beef broth

1½ cups low-sodium chicken broth

ROAST DIRECTIONS: Toast unpeeled garlic cloves in a small skillet over medium heat, tossing frequently, about 8 minutes. When cool enough to handle, peel cloves and cut into ¼-inch silvers. Using a sharp paring knife, make 1-inch deep slits all over roast. Insert toasted garlic slivers into the slits.

RUB DIRECTIONS: Mix minced garlic, thyme and salt together in small bowl. Rub all over garlic studded roast. Place roast on large plate and refrigerate, uncovered, at least 4 hours or overnight.

GARLIC PASTE DIRECTIONS: Heat halved garlic cloves, thyme, bay leaves, salt and oil in a small saucepan over medium heat for about 2 to 3 minutes. Reduce heat to low and cook until garlic is soft, about 30 minutes. Cool. Strain, reserving garlic-flavored oil and the garlic cloves. Discard herbs. Transfer to a small bowl. Mash garlic with 1 tablespoon "garlic-flavored" oil until a paste forms. Cover and refrigerate garlic paste and the remaining garlic oil until ready to use. Using paper towels, wipe garlic-salt rub off beef. Rub beef with 2 tablespoons reserved garlic oil and season with pepper. Allow beef to set at room temperature for 30 minutes.

Meanwhile, adjust oven rack to middle position, place roasting pan on rack and preheat oven to 450°F.

Transfer beef, fat side down, to preheated roasting pan and place in oven. Roast beef until browned on all sides, by turning to sear, about 10 to 15 minutes.

Reduce oven temperature to 300°F. Remove roasting pan from oven. Turn roast fat side up and coat top of roast with garlic paste. Return meat to oven and roast until internal temperature reaches to 130°F on food thermometer, about 50 to 70 minutes. Transfer to cutting board; cover loosely with foil. Allow to rest 20 to 25 minutes. Meanwhile prepare the au jus.

AU JUS DIRECTIONS: Drain excess fat from roasting pan and place pan over high heat. Add broths and bring to boil, using wooden spoon to scrape browned pieces from bottom of pan. Simmer, stirring until reduced to 2 cups, about 15 minutes. Add juices from beef roast and cook about 1 minute. Pour through strainer. Discard solids. Slice beef crosswise against grain into ¼-inch slices. Serve with au jus.
Makes 10 to 12 servings.

NOTE: Other cuts of beef that can be used: eye of round roast, bottom round roast, and chuck center roast

—— *From Our Family Album* ——

Today's Easter traditions involve an egg hunt as well as a scavenger hunt at Grandma Judy and Grandpa Lary's home at Eckert's Millstadt Farm. Each child hunts for a specific color of egg so there are no arguments, and for the scavenger hunt, the kids form teams with a variety of ages on each, and then search the farm for hidden treasures. Grandma Judy's riddles are tricky, which keeps the kids on their toes!

Butterflied Oven-Roasted Herb Chicken

5 garlic cloves, peeled

4 Tbs. snipped flat-leaf parsley

2 Tbs. snipped fresh thyme or 2 tsp dried

2 Tbs. snipped fresh rosemary or 1 tsp. dried

Zest of 1 lemon

Salt and pepper

¼ cup extra-virgin olive oil

1 whole chicken, washed and patted dry

Preheat oven to 450°F. In a food processor, combine garlic, parsley, thyme, rosemary, lemon zest and 1 teaspoon salt. Once combined, drizzle in 3 tablespoons olive oil and process until a coarse paste forms.

Gently slide your fingers between the skin and flesh of the chicken breasts and legs. Place breast side down on a cutting board, with the large cavity facing you. Using kitchen shears, start at the open cavity and cut down each side of the backbone; discard the backbone. Open the chicken like a book, and then flip over. Press down firmly on the top fleshy part of the breast until you hear the bone crack.

Using your fingers, stuff the herb mixture under the skin, spreading it evenly. Rub the remaining 1 tablespoon olive oil on the skin and underside of the chicken; season with salt and pepper. Place breast side up in a roasting pan and cook until the skin is golden and crispy or until an instant-read thermometer registers an internal temperature of 165°F, about 45 minutes.

During the last 10 minutes, cover loosely with foil. Let the chicken rest for 15 minutes before carving. Makes 4 servings.

DESSERTS

— *From Our Family Album* —

During the remodeling process of the store and restaurant in 2010, the family adamantly preserved Alvin Eckert's original store. Today Alvin's historic structure stands within the expanded dining rooms of Eckert's Country Restaurant.

Oven Rhubarb Brown Betty

1 cup panko bread crumbs

¼ cup plus 2 Tbs. packed light brown sugar

⅔ cup plus ¼ cup granulated sugar

1½ tsp. ground cinnamon

½ tsp. ground allspice

¼ tsp. ground ginger

Pinch of ground cloves

About 4 cups rhubarb, peeled, trim top and bottom, cut into 1 inch pieces

1 tsp. fresh lemon juice

½ cup roughly chopped almonds, optional

4 Tbs. cold unsalted butter, cut into small pieces, plus 1 Tbs. more for baking pan

9 scoops Eckert's Frozen Custard

Preheat oven to 350°F. Whisk the panko, 2 tablespoons brown sugar, ¼ cup granulated sugar, cinnamon, allspice, ginger and cloves in a medium bowl until combined. Set aside. In another bowl, toss the rhubarb with the remaining ¼ cup brown sugar, ⅔ cup granulated sugar and the lemon juice to coat. Butter a shallow 8-inch square glass baking dish. Sprinkle 3 tablespoons of the breadcrumb mixture in the bottom of the dish. Top with the rhubarb, then sprinkle with the remaining crumbs and the almonds. Dot with the cut-up butter. Bake until the filling is bubbly and topping is golden brown and crisp, 30 to 35 minutes. Let cool, about 15 to 20 minutes. Serve warm topped with Eckert's Frozen Custard. Makes 9 servings.

Dip Your Own Fresh Strawberry Dip

2 pints strawberries with stems
½ cup dairy sour cream
½ cup lightly packed brown sugar

Wash and dry berries. Set aside. Spoon sour cream and sugar into separate small bowls. Place bowls on a large serving platter. Arrange strawberries around bowls. To eat, first dip berries in sour cream then in brown sugar. Makes 4 to 6 servings.

Grilled Pound Cake with Warm Berry Sauce

3 heaping cups mixed berries, such as strawberries, blueberries, and blackberries
Juice ½ a lemon
2 Tbs. granulated sugar, divided
¼ cup plus 1 Tbs. water
¼ tsp. vanilla extract
1½ tsp. cornstarch
1 Eckert's Pound Cake or Pound Cake recipe on 77, cut into 10 to 12 slices
4 Tbs. unsalted melted butter

In a medium saucepan over medium-low heat, combine the berries, lemon juice, 1 tablespoon of granulated sugar, ¼ cup water, and vanilla. Cook covered until the berries are softened, about 5 minutes. Partially mash the berries. Taste and add remaining granulated sugar if the mixture is tart. Set aside. In a small bowl, stir 1 tablespoon of water into cornstarch, then stir the cornstarch mixture into the warm berry sauce and continue cooking, uncovered, until thickened, 2 to 3 minutes. Remove from heat and cover to keep warm. Preheat grill or broiler to medium low heat. Brush the pound cake slices with melted butter. Grill until the cake is toasted, about 2 minutes on each side. Spread the warm sauce on the dessert plates. Place 2 cake slices on each plate, and top with additional sauce. Makes 5 to 6 servings.

Strawberry Lemon Trifle

½ cup Eckert's strawberry preserves

¼ cup water

2 cups heavy cream, chilled

1 cup lemon curd at room temperature

12 sponge cake shells, Eckert's Pound Cake, Angel Food Cake or Strawberry & Cream Cake (cut into 12 slices)

4 to 6 cups strawberries, washed, hulled and cut in half

In a small microwavable bowl, stir together the jam and water. Microwave for 1 minute at full power. Stir until slightly cool. Using an electric mixer, beat cream at medium-high speed until stiff. Using a rubber spatula, fold in the lemon curd until well incorporated. Cut the cake shells in half to form semicircles. Place 6 halves in an even layer in the bottom of a 10 cup trifle bowl. Drizzle half of the melted jam mixture onto the cake. Spoon ½ of the lemon cream on top and spread evenly. Layer ½ of berries on the lemon cream. Spread evenly. Repeat the layering once more, mounding the last batch of berries in the center of the trifle. Makes 10 to 12 servings.

Strawberry Rhubarb Crumbed-Top Pie

1⅓ cups granulated sugar

⅓ cup flour

2 cups strawberries, hulled and sliced

2 cups rhubarb, chopped into 1 inch pieces

1 (9-inch) unbaked pie shell

2 Tbs. butter, cut into pieces

CRUMB TOPPING

1 cup flour

⅓ cup granulated sugar

½ tsp. cinnamon

¼ tsp. salt

½ cup cold butter, cut into pieces

GLAZE

1 tsp. water

1 Tbs. powdered sugar, sifted

Preheat oven to 375°F. In a medium bowl, combine granulated sugar and flour and set aside. In a large mixing bowl combine strawberries and rhubarb; add sugar/flour mixture to fruit. Pour contents into pie shell and dot with butter. To prepare crumb topping: in a medium bowl combine flour, granulated sugar, cinnamon, and salt. Cut butter into mixture until topping is crumbly. Sprinkle topping over top of fruit. Bake for 20 minutes: reduce temperature to 350°F and continue to bake until rhubarb is tender when tested with a toothpick or the point of a paring knife. To prepare glaze: combine water with powdered sugar and mix well; drizzle glaze over top of pie. Makes 6 servings.

Strawberry Swirl Cheesecake

CRUST
1½ cups chocolate wafer crumbs
¼ cup butter; softened, plus 2 Tbs. for pan

STRAWBERRY SWIRL
2 cups strawberries, hulled and sliced
½ cup granulated sugar
2 Tbs. cornstarch

FILLING
4 (8 oz.) pkgs cream cheese, softened
1½ cups granulated sugar
4 large eggs
1 Tbs. fresh lemon juice
1 tsp. vanilla extract

TOPPING
4 cups whole strawberries, hulled

Preheat oven to 350°F. Grease a 9-inch spring form pan with 2 tablespoons butter. Set aside. To prepare crust: in a bowl, combine butter and wafer crumbs until crumbly. Press into bottom and partway up the sides of pan. Chill for 1 hour. To prepare strawberry swirl: puree strawberries in a blender or food processor. In a medium saucepan combine granulated sugar and cornstarch and stir in strawberry puree. Bring to a boil over medium heat and cook for 2 minutes, stirring constantly; cool to room temperature.

TO PREPARE FILLING: in a large mixing bowl, beat cream cheese on medium with electric mixer until smooth; gradually beat in granulated sugar, eggs, lemon juice, and vanilla. Pour ½ of cream cheese batter into cold chocolate crumb crust. Spoon strawberry swirl mixture in dollops on top of batter. With end of wooden spoon gently swirl together to "marbleize." Top with remaining batter, spreading evenly. Bake for 45 to 50 minutes, or until cake is just set in the center; place on wire rack to cool completely. To serve, top with strawberries. Makes 12 to 14 servings.

Strawberry-Rhubarb Cobbler

FILLING

4 pints or 8 cups strawberries, hulled and thickly sliced

2 cups rhubarb, trimmed and cut into ½-inch pieces

½ cup granulated sugar

2 Tbs. quick-cooking tapioca or 1 Tbs. cornstarch

⅛ tsp. ground cinnamon

⅛ tsp. ground ginger

⅛ tsp. ground nutmeg

TOPPING

1½ cups flour

¼ cup plus 1 Tbs. granulated sugar, divided

1½ tsp. baking powder

½ tsp. baking soda

½ tsp. salt

¼ tsp. ground cinnamon

¼ tsp. ground ginger

¼ tsp. ground nutmeg

2 Tbs. cold butter, cut into pieces

1 cup nonfat buttermilk

TO PREPARE FILLING: Combine strawberries, rhubarb, sugar, tapioca or cornstarch, ginger, cinnamon and nutmeg in a 9-inch deep-dish pie pan and let stand for 20 minutes.

TO PREPARE TOPPING: Preheat oven to 400°F. Stir together flour, ¼ cup granulated sugar, baking powder, baking soda, salt, cinnamon, ginger and nutmeg in a large bowl. Cut butter into dry ingredients with a pastry cutter, 2 forks or fingers until crumbly. Using a fork, stir in buttermilk just until combined. Using a large spoon, drop the dough in 8 dollops over the filling. Sprinkle with remaining 1 tablespoon sugar. Bake cobbler until browned and bubbling, 40 to 50 minutes. Cover with foil if the top is browning too quickly. Cool slightly on a wire rack. Cool 20 to 45 minutes before serving.
Makes 8 servings.

From Our Kitchen

To make your own buttermilk or "sour milk," mix 1 tablespoon lemon juice or vinegar to 1 cup milk. Allow mixture to sit for a few minutes at room temperature. Then proceed with your recipe.

Ruth's Glazed Strawberry Pie

2 quarts (8 cups) strawberries, hulled and divided
1 cup granulated sugar
4 Tbs. cornstarch
1 tsp. lemon juice
1 (9-inch) baked pie shell
Whipped cream for garnish

Using a potato masher, crush 2 cups of berries in a saucepan. In a small bowl, combine granulated sugar and cornstarch; add to crushed berries. Cook and stir 4 to 5 minutes over medium heat until thick and clear. Add lemon juice. Cool. Cut remaining berries in halves and add to cooled mixture. Pour into baked pie shell and chill at least 2 hours. Top with whipped cream and serve. Makes 6 servings.

Fresh Strawberry Cream Pie

4 oz. cream cheese, softened
¼ cup dairy sour cream
1 (9-inch) baked pie shell
1 to 1½ qts. hulled strawberries, divided
1 cup granulated sugar
3 Tbs. cornstarch
½ cup water

In a 2 quart bowl, beat cream cheese until fluffy; add sour cream and beat until smooth, about 1 minute. Spread mixture on bottom of cooked pie shell and refrigerate while cooking filling. Crush enough berries to make 1 cup. In a small bowl, mix granulated sugar and cornstarch together. In a saucepan, add water, crushed berries and sugar/cornstarch mixture. Cook and stir over medium heat until mixture is clear and has thickened, about 2 to 3 minutes. Remove from heat and cool for at least 10 minutes. Top cream cheese mixture with remaining berries (tips up) and pour cooked berry mixture over top. Chill at least 1 hour before serving. Makes 6 to 7 servings.

Pound Cake

3 cups granulated sugar
1 cup butter, softened
6 large eggs, separated
3 cups flour
¼ tsp. baking powder
1 cup (8 oz.) dairy sour cream
1 Tbs. butter
1 to 2 Tbs. flour for pan

Preheat oven to 300°F. In a large mixing bowl, cream granulated sugar and butter together about 2 to 3 minutes. Add egg yolks, one at a time, creaming after each addition. In a medium bowl, combine flour and baking powder and add to creamed mixture alternately with sour cream. In a separate bowl, beat egg whites until stiff and fold into batter. Pour into a greased and floured 10 to 12 cup tube pan. Bake for 1½ hours or until a toothpick inserted into cake comes out clean. Place on a wire cooling rack. Allow to cool 10 to 15 minutes. Remove cake from pan. Cool before slicing. Makes 10 to 12 servings.

Juanita's Speedy Sponge Cake

2 large eggs
1 cup granulated sugar
1 cup flour
1 tsp. baking powder
⅛ tsp. salt
½ cup hot milk, not boiling
1 Tbs. butter, melted
1 tsp. vanilla extract

Preheat oven to 350°F. In a small bowl, beat eggs until light and thick, 5 to 6 minutes. Slowly add granulated sugar and continue beating for 2½ minutes. Fold in flour, baking powder and salt all at once. Add milk, butter and vanilla and mix well. Pour into a greased and floured 8x8 baking pan. Bake for 30 minutes or until top is golden brown. Makes 9 servings.

NOTE: The secret to perfect texture in this recipe is beating the eggs for 5 to 6 minutes.

Eckert's Rhubarb Custard Pie

1 unbaked Eckert's Frozen 9-inch pie crust
1 cup rhubarb, thin sliced in ½ inch pieces
3 large eggs, slightly beaten
¼ cup brown sugar
¾ cup granulated sugar
1 cup milk
1 tsp. pure vanilla extract
Dash of cinnamon
Dash of nutmeg

Preheat oven to 400°F. Partially bake pie crust for 6 to 8 minutes. Remove from oven. Place rhubarb pieces on top of the partially baked pie crust. In a medium bowl, whisk eggs, sugars, milk, vanilla, and spices together. Pour mixture over the rhubarb. Bake for 35 minutes or until custard is just set on top. Allow pie to rest for 10 to 15 minutes before cutting. Cool fully, cover and refrigerate if not serving immediately. Makes 6 to 8 servings.

Eckert's Spring Fruit Dessert Squares

CRUST
½ Tbs butter
1 cup flour
⅓ cup confectioners' sugar
3 Tbs. cornstarch
¼ tsp. salt
5 Tbs. butter, softened

FRUIT
2 cups strawberries, hulled and sliced
2 cups rhubarb, peeled and thinly chopped
⅓ cup water
1 Tbs. lemon juice

FILLING
2 large eggs, lightly beaten
⅓ cup granulated sugar
3 Tbs. cornstarch
¼ tsp. salt
9 hulled strawberries for garnish
2 Tbs. confectioners' sugar for garnish

Preheat oven to 350°F. Line an 8-inch square glass baking dish with foil and butter the foil. Combine flour, confectioners' sugar, cornstarch and salt in a medium bowl. Add butter and blend into the flour mixture with 2 forks until evenly combined. The mixture will be crumbly. Firmly press the crust mixture into the prepared pan. Bake until just barely beginning to brown, about 15 to 20 minutes.

TO PREPARE FRUIT: Combine strawberries, rhubarb, ⅓ cup water and lemon juice in a medium saucepan. Cook over high heat, stirring, until the fruit is tender, about 4 to 6 minutes. Pour through a fine-mesh sieve and press on the solids to extract all the juices; discard solids. Pour strained juice into a measuring cup; remove any extra or add a little water to make 1 cup of liquid.

TO PREPARE FILLING: Whisk eggs in a medium bowl. Add sugar, cornstarch and salt. Stir in 1 cup of fruit juice mixture. Pour the filling over the crust. Bake until just set, about 15 to 20 minutes. The center will be somewhat loose and will firm up as it cools. Let cool to room temperature, about 1½ hours. Using the edges of foil, gently lift out the baked dessert all in one piece. Cut into 9 inch squares. Garnish with fresh strawberries and dust with confectioners' sugar. Makes 9 squares.

Roasted Strawberries with Black Pepper, Balsamic Vinegar, and Mascarpone Cheese

20 to 24 whole large strawberries, stem on

2 Tbs. light brown sugar

1 Tbs. white balsamic vinegar

1 8 oz. mascarpone cheese

Fresh cracked black pepper

6 slices Eckert's Irish Soda Bread

Fresh mint leaves, finely minced, optional

Preheat oven to 400°F. Place strawberries on a rimmed sheet pan. Bake 8 minutes or until juice runs and the color darkens. Remove stem and caps. Place hot strawberries in a medium bowl. Add brown sugar and vinegar and gently toss. Set aside for 5 to 10 minutes. Lightly toast Irish Soda Bread and cut each piece into thirds. Mix mascarpone cheese with fresh cracked black pepper, (about ½ teaspoon or to your taste). Spread a thin layer of cheese on toasted bread. Top each with roasted strawberries and some juice. Makes 9 servings (1½ to 1¾ cups of roasted berries and juice).

From Our Kitchen

The trick to preserving strawberry juices during roasting, is keeping the stem intact. Do not hull strawberries before the roasting step or your juices will seep out the stem end.

Fresh Strawberry Yogurt Cake

2½ cups flour, divided
½ tsp. baking soda
½ tsp. salt
Zest of one lemon
1 cup (2 sticks) butter, softened
2 cups granulated sugar
3 large eggs
3 Tbs. lemon juice, divided
8 oz. plain or vanilla Greek yogurt
12 oz. fresh strawberries, diced
1 cup powdered sugar

Preheat oven to 375°F. Grease and flour a 10 inch Bundt pan (10 to 15 cup pan). Sift together 2¼ cups of flour, baking soda and salt. Mix in the lemon zest and set aside. With an electric mixer, cream together the butter and granulated sugar until light and fluffy. Beat in the eggs one at a time, then mix in 1 tablespoon lemon juice. Alternate beating in the flour/zest mixture and the yogurt, mixing just until incorporated. Toss the strawberries with the remaining ¼ cup of flour. Gently fold them into the batter. Pour the batter into the Bundt pan. Place in the oven and reduce the temperature to 325°F. Bake for 60 minutes, or until a toothpick inserted into the center of the cake comes out clean. Allow to cool at least 20 minutes in the pan, then turn out onto a wire rack and cool completely. Once cake is cooled, whisk together the remaining 2 tablespoons of lemon juice and powdered sugar. Drizzle over the top of the cake.
Makes 12 to 14 servings.

Chilled Strawberry Cream

2 cups fresh, unsweetened whole
strawberries
¼ cup powdered sugar
½ cup heavy whipping cream

Place the strawberries and sugar in a food processor; cover and process until finely chopped. In a small bowl, beat cream until stiff peaks form. Fold into berries. Pour into serving dishes. Refrigerate or freeze for 25 minutes. Use as icing or as a topping for fresh sliced strawberries and pound cake. Makes 2 servings.

Eckert's Strawberry Buttercream Frosting

¾ cup strawberries, sliced
¾ cup butter, softened
1 (32 oz.) package powdered sugar

Process strawberries in blender or food processor until pureed (puree should measure about ½ cup). Beat butter at medium speed with electric mixer until creamy; gradually add powdered sugar alternately with pureed strawberries, beating until well blended after addition of strawberries. Makes 5 to 6 cups.

Grandma's Egg Custard Pie

1 Eckert's unbaked pie shell
1 egg white
2½ cups milk
3 large eggs, beaten
¾ cup granulated sugar
¼ tsp. salt
1 tsp. vanilla extract
¼ tsp. fresh grated nutmeg

Preheat oven to 400°F. Brush inside of pie crust with egg white to help prevent crust from getting soggy. Scald milk by pouring it into a medium, heavy bottomed pot. Place pot over medium heat. Watch pot and stir periodically. Once bubbles start to form around the edges, read temperature. Milk is considered scalded when it hits just below the boiling point (approximately 212°F). Cool milk to approximately 100°F before proceeding. In a medium bowl, whisk together 3 eggs, granulated sugar, salt, and vanilla. Pour milk into bowl and mix well. Pour liquid into pie crust (you may have more liquid than you need to fill the crust). Grate nutmeg over the top of the pie. Bake 40 to 50 minutes or until a knife inserted near the center comes out clean. Cool before serving. Store remaining servings in refrigerator.
Makes 6 to 8 servings.

Honey Strawberry Yogurt Parfait

⅓ cup Eckert's Pure Honey

3 cups plain yogurt or Greek yogurt

1 tsp. vanilla extract

2 to 3 cups strawberries, hulled and chopped

½ cup granola

6 large whole strawberries

Stir together honey, yogurt, and vanilla. Alternate layers of yogurt mixture and strawberries in 6 glasses. Top with granola. Garnish with whole strawberries. Makes 6 servings.

—— *From Our Family Album* ——

Grandma Eckert was an avid vegetable gardener. She squared off her garden and its rows with sticks and string. She marked each row with a seed packet that hung on a stick.

ECKERT'S FAMILY HISTORY

Today, the sixth and seventh generations oversee the daily operations of the Eckert farms. The current Eckert orchard business began in 1837 when Johann Peter Eckert landed in Pittsburgh, Pennsylvania, from Dietzenbach, Hesse Darmestadt, Germany, with his wife and four sons. As German tradition would have it, Johann Peter farmed and eventually bought each of his sons a farm. Johann's son Michael followed his instinctive love for the land and lived on the farm we now call Drum Hill, near Fayetteville, Illinois.

The first fruit trees were planted on Michael Eckert's farm in 1862. Michael had three children, but only one son, Henry, lived to adulthood. After his marriage in 1877, Henry built the present Eckert home on Turkey Hill, just outside of Belleville, in 1880. The first fruit trees were planted on Turkey Hill in 1890. Henry and Mary Eckert had three sons and a daughter; their daughter died in infancy. Their youngest son, Alvin O., married Ella Heinrich and resided in the family home where they raised three sons, Cornell, Curt, and Vernon.

The Turkey Hill Farm today is what we call our Belleville farm. The first roadside farm stand was opened on Turkey Hill by Alvin O. in 1910 and became the nucleus of our growing business. All three sons majored in agriculture at the University of Illinois and returned home after graduation to turn the business into a father-sons partnership.

Today, Jim Eckert, son of Juanita and Vernon, is president of Eckert Orchards and is the company's chief horticulturist. Lary Eckert, son of Curt and Ruth, recently resigned as president of Eckert's, Inc., after presiding over the company for 30 years. Lary's son, Chris Eckert, succeeded him as president. Chris oversees retail operations, as well as the growing and wholesaling of homegrown products. Additionally, Lary's daughter, Jill Eckert-Tantillo, is vice president of Marketing and Food Services. Angie Eckert, Chris's wife, is vice president of Retail Operations for both the Country Store and the Garden Center.

Index of Recipes